Merry

CW00410398

To Zonya,

Hope you have a lovely
Christmas!

Lots of love,
Lesley xxx

Published by Association of Christian Writers
www.christianwriters.org.uk

Copyright © Individual Authors

All rights reserved. No part of this publication may be
reproduced, stored or transmitted in any form, or by any
means electronic, mechanical, or photocopying, recording or
otherwise, without the prior permission of the copyright owner.

All Bible Verses are from the ESV.

Cover design by Cathy Helms of Avalon Graphics

ISBN 978-1-9999581-2-1

Merry Christmas, Everyone

A festive feast of Stories, Poems and Reflections

EDITED BY

Wendy H Jones
Amy Robinson
Jane Clamp

To

ALL MEMBERS

of the

Association of Christian Writers

Each and every one of you is valued, but only so many could be included in this book. We are proud to be able to represent such a highly talented group of writers.

 Contents

The Birth

Animals and Shepherds

❄

In the Inn

Following the Star

FIRESIDE STORIES
Curl up for a cosy read

I WONDER AS I WANDER
Seasonal Memories and Musings

Tinsel and Turkey
All the Trimmings of Christmas

Light in the Darkness
Christmas When Times are Tough

FOR GOD SO LOVED THE WORLD
Christmas in Every Nation

AND FINALLY

Foreword

WHAT a feast! Here is a celebration of the Incarnation: origins, stories, customs, memories, current festivities. Characters from the biblical accounts feature prominently, as you would expect, but so do people of today—noisy and exhausting but infinitely welcome returning families, a gentleman of the road, orphaned children dignified despite their circumstances.

The Incarnation is where heaven and earth interfold and overlap. ACW's gifted writers have placed their imaginations at the service of the Most High, to explore with delight and fervour what it can mean to encounter Jesus: in the stable, or the kitchen, or a foreign land.

It is easy to speak of Jesus. Preachers do it every week, it's their job. All good preachers know it is much harder to speak with honesty, because crafting words which contain the truth of lived experience, of personal engagement and troubling discovery, is always demanding and often painful. These monologues, narratives, songs, poems and sketches are authentic, because every piece has arisen from a writer sending out their spirit in prayer and reflection, then distilling her or his encounter with the divine into articulate form.

It takes a special persistence to write well. It's partly about looking within, flinching but continuing to observe, allowing light to penetrate and choosing to notice the results. It's partly about keeping going, wrestling intractable impressions and half-perceived apprehensions into crisp fluidity, like finely-carved stonework. It's partly about being able to conceive both the detail and the whole, which takes some mental heavy lifting. It's partly about exposing, repeatedly, your carefully-crafted oeuvre to the dim light of others' indifference. The delicacy and trauma of human experience are not easily translated into words worth reading, and a writer's life can be gruelling.

Yet, when idea and expression coincide, what a durable delight is generated. May this collection be a channel of grace to you, and provide a heightened awareness of the season in which we celebrate God becoming human.

Tony Collins
SPCK

Introduction

IT is a delight to write the introduction to *Merry Christmas, Everyone*, an anthology which has been edited by Amy Robinson, Wendy Jones and Jane Clamp, all members of the ACW committee. They have been instrumental in drawing together contributions from many ACW writers, some of whom have never been published before.

When you turn to the contents page you will find an impressive number of items. The contributions range from essays, devotionals, poems and stories to a single beautiful carol, complete with how to access its music. All this has been ably put together with the help and expert knowledge of Adrianne Fitzpatrick who founded the publishing house, Books to Treasure. Our thanks go to those on the committee who assisted in reading, selecting and proofreading entries.

Readers who belong to the Association of Christian Writers will know that we aim to inspire, encourage and equip Christians who write. In today's competitive writing world, it can be difficult to have one's work published, so this book will help many members on their writing journey. The Association also offers information about writing on our members' website, a blog that anyone can access, plus writers' days, writers' groups and the excellent quarterly magazine, *Christian Writer*, which members receive.

ACW is not a publishing house, so the two publications this year (a Lent book and this present anthology) are rare forays into the publishing world. Although there is unlikely to be another collaborative publication for a while, there will be competitions to enter plus opportunities relating to our grand 50th Anniversary celebrations in 2021.

Meanwhile, whether you have received the anthology as a gift, bought it for yourself or are one of the writers within its pages, take time for yourself amongst the busyness of Christmas to relax with a mince pie and drink to hand, to savour the rich feast that is within these covers.

Be blessed this Christmas,

Angela Hobday
Chair, Association of Christian Writers

Using the pen-name Annie Try, Angela Hobday writes thought-provoking novels with a touch of mystery. She is now working on the third Dr Mike Lewis story; the first two titles Trying to Fly *and* Out of Silence *were published in 2017 by Instant Apostle.*

Acknowledgements

Thanks go to

JANE BROCKLEHURST and MARION OSGOOD
for all their hard work in proofreading this book.
For this we are truly grateful.

Advent

Readings about preparation and waiting

Prima Gravida

Ann Bodimeade

THEY say that God always answers prayer, but not necessarily in the way that we expect. So I have tried to accept that God's answer to our prayer for a child was 'No'. Zechariah accepted it long ago and tried to reassure me. He's a good man; some men would have divorced me and taken a younger wife, but not Zechariah: he accepted that it was not God's will for him to be a father and carried on serving, faithfully, as a priest and praying for God to save His people.

I've sometimes wondered if Zechariah is relieved not to have brought a child into a country under Roman occupation. We may be able to practise our religion, for now, and we don't see much of the Roman army up here in the hill country, but people are restless and Roman punishments are harsh and cruel. I know Zechariah believes that God will rescue us. He knows the Scriptures and that God has always saved his people, but he also knows that you can't hurry God. So he continues to pray for God to rescue His people just as I, quietly, continued to pray for a child.

Even so it must have come as a shock to him when an angel appeared and told him our prayers had been heard. Well, it was such a shock he was speechless, literally struck dumb. He hasn't said a word since. He came back from the Temple and when I saw him I just knew. He signed to me that our prayers had been answered but I already knew that somehow, miraculously, we would have a child. I could have danced for joy and shouted it from the rooftops but I didn't. I stayed indoors, partly because a first-time mum at my age provokes too much curiosity, but mainly because I didn't want to do anything to risk losing this precious gift.

Then I heard about young Mary, that she had seen an angel too. What can I say? Miracles happen! I had to believe her, but not everyone did. I'm not even sure that her parents believed her. Her fiancé said he would stand by her; her father said, 'And so he should.' He may not have believed about the angel but he couldn't believe his daughter had been unfaithful to Joseph. I invited her to come and stay with me for a while, away from the gossip. It's nice for me to have someone to talk to since Zechariah is silent and whether you are a prima gravida at fifteen or fifty-one it's still a first pregnancy.

When I saw her, I wondered how anyone could doubt her story. The Holy Spirit shone from her and my baby turned somersaults in my womb. Such maturity in so young a body. She radiated peace and seemed to know that although her path would not be easy, God was with her. I found that her prayer had been 'Yes' to God, not from naivety, but from a deep faith.

It was then I knew that prayers are answered, but not necessarily when we want or as we expect. The angel told Zechariah our prayers had been heard. And they have been answered: mine for a child and his for the salvation of our nation.

Ann Bodimeade is a wife, mother, Spiritual Accompanier and swimmer. She has written dramas and a pantomime for her church and now writes a blog and for the parish magazine as Swimming Pilgrim.

When the Time had Fully Come

Janet Killeen

An indrawn breath of waiting.
Imminence so close, so urgent,
Resembling blood, throbbing in the heart,
Beating in the throat.
Reverberating silently for those with ears to hear.

Like a quickening in her own long-widowed womb,
A word upholds her now, watchful for his coming.
And an old man, sleepless with longing, raises
Eager eyes to heaven.

Far away, a gathering of the wise
Has searched the skies for guidance
Exceeding all their past predictions
Of this vast sweep of dazzling constellations.

The imperial seal is pressed into ready wax.
A hundred emissaries ride to command a census.
In far-off provinces, indifferent to Rome,
Wearied people shrug and stir,
Beginning journeys that return them to their birth.

In his palace a king stares into the shadowed corners
Of his mind, demanding light
To banish darkness and its terrors,

Fearing to eat the poisoned fruit that he himself has sown.
Among their restless flock, heavy now with lamb,
Shepherds listen for that first tremulous bleat of birth
And watch and wait for dawn to dull the stars,
Ushering the sun over the eastern hills.

And in a northern town, an anxious husband watches
His young wife smooth and fold some linen strips into their pack
Before her slow and gravid steps
Will take her south beside him.

Janet Killeen has been writing short stories and poetry since her retirement from teaching ten years ago; she published her first novel, After the Flood *in 2017. She writes to engage with questions of faith and reconciliation, choice and suffering, and always with a perspective of hope.*

Baby's First Christmas

K A Hitchins

IT was nearly Christmas. Expectation floated in the night air, mingling with the smell of spices, jingling with the ring of camel harnesses.

Baby Jesus entered the darkness.

'Have you seen my beautiful star?' he asked the caravan train. 'I threw it into the sky—high up so you couldn't miss it.'

'Yes,' the wise men said, stroking their beards and squinting up at the heavens. 'We've just pointed it out to Herod.'

'That old killjoy!' Baby Jesus frowned. 'I'll be bumping into his offspring later to grant his Christmas wish. But in the meantime, did you bring my presents?'

The magi nodded and patted their saddle bags. Baby Jesus was breathless with excitement.

'Don't forget to put them under the manger. I'll be putting my gift on a tree.'

It was nearly Christmas. Anticipation prickled as families travelled home like flocks of migrating birds. Children grizzled. Fathers whistled. Crowded roadsides bubbled and sizzled like the fat in the innkeeper's pan.

Baby Jesus knocked on the door.

'Are my mummy and daddy here yet?'

'Who are you? How should I know? This place is heaving,' the innkeeper snapped.

'You'll know them when you see them,' Baby Jesus said. 'Mummy's the one in the blue dress and the big tummy. And Daddy will be lighting up the night with starlight and angels.'

Grumpy and overworked, the innkeeper shook his head. 'If they haven't got a reservation, I've got no room.'

'When they get here, don't forget you have a stable out the back. I don't mind laying my head in a borrowed place ... Oh! And I'll need some white strips of linen to swaddle my body.'

The innkeeper wiped his greasy hands on his apron. 'I'm coming,' he shouted to the hungry guests indoors, and shut the door on Baby Jesus.

It was nearly Christmas. Whiskered shepherds, enfolded by shrouds of night, snoozed on the hillside. Whispering angels unfolded wings of light and hid behind the clouds, waiting for their moment to jump out and shout, 'Surprise!'

Baby Jesus gathered up the lambs.

'Have the angels come yet?'

The shepherds rubbed their sleepy faces and wondered what he was talking about.

'When they get here, come and find me, then run and tell everyone that the angels said, "Jesus is alive!"'

It was nearly Christmas. A million stars twinkled down on a world wrapped in darkness, ribboned with pain. A great hush fell, a sudden intake of breath as hope sneaked into a dusty corner. Exhaustion burned behind the eyes of the Kings and Shepherds, and tugged at the Innkeeper's apron. It weighed down the feet of a donkey, as Mary and Joseph—hearts filled with angel dust—carried a treasure to Bethlehem.

It was far too early in the morning to unwrap a gift, but Baby Jesus looked at the world he had been planning to enter for thousands of years and beamed at his earthly parents.

'You're here! It's time! Let Christmas begin!'

Kathryn Hitchins writes contemporary fiction from a faith perspective. The Girl at the End of the Road *was published in March 2016 by* Instant Apostle. The Key of All Unknown *(finalist,* Woman Alive Magazine's Readers' Choice Award 2017*) followed in October 2016.* The Gardener's Daughter *was released on 15 March 2018. Kathryn was also a contributor to the* ACW Lent Book New Life: Reflections for Lent *(www.kahitchins.co.uk)*

A Part to Play

Lesley Crawford

THE final audience member arrived just in time. As I directed them to their seat, the orchestra had already begun to tune, and I managed to exit into the foyer just as the house lights dimmed and the overture began. Captivated by the music, I paused. There was work to get on with, but first I had to stay for a few moments and listen—just to the overture.

Pressing my face up close to the window on the auditorium door, I watched and listened, fascinated by the different instruments and how they played together: the delicate melody on the violins, the rich harmony of the violas and cellos supporting it, the driving rhythm of the double bass underpinning it all. Everything was perfectly balanced.

As the volume increased and the woodwind section entered, my attention was drawn straightaway to the clarinet. That was my instrument and I knew the part so well that my fingers automatically began to move in the familiar patterns of the phrases being played.

I loved to listen, but the music also filled me with an almost painful longing to be part of it. I didn't want to be standing here, a spectator on the other side of the door; I longed to take my place in the orchestra and join in with the music. I was only fifteen years old and I knew it was too early. I knew there was a good chance that in a few years my time would come but, for now, I was excluded, on the other side of the door.

Suddenly, I noticed that I was no longer alone. The lady who led the front-of-house team had joined me by the auditorium door and, as I looked at her face, I saw my own desire mirrored there and realised that she, too, longed to be part of the orchestra. The difference was that for her it was not a hope for the future, but the reality of the past. I knew that she had once been a professional musician and had taken her place on the other side of the door; now that age and arthritis had taken their toll and she would never play at that level again. Like me, she was excluded, watching from the side-lines, longing to participate. We stood silently as the overture continued, somehow united in our unspoken longings; then, as the final cadence sounded, we shared a smile. Letting go of our hopes for the future and our memories of the past, we returned our focus to the present and went to get on with our work.

As I remember that moment, it brings to mind two ladies we meet in the Christmas Story.

For Elizabeth, it was too late. She and her husband, Zechariah, had tried for children for several years, with no success. Now time had run out and she was too old. It was impossible.

For Mary, it was too early. She was too young. She and Joseph were engaged, but not yet married. For her, the thought of children was far off in the future. Maybe one day, but the idea that she would have one now? It was impossible. And yet, with God, nothing is impossible, and, for him, the time was right.

Two angelic visits, two baby boys—and not just any baby boys, but baby boys with wonderful destinies. One to prepare the way and turn people's hearts to God, the other to save and to reign forever: God's own son, Emmanuel, God with us. It seemed impossible, but nothing is impossible with God, and these two women, who would have been dismissed by others as too young or too old, were exactly right for God and were chosen to play vital parts in his plan.

Lesley Crawford lives in Scotland, works for a Christian charity, and enjoys playing music in her spare time as part of a wind band and an orchestra. She blogs at www.lifeinthespaciousplace.wordpress.com and she is also a regular contributor at www.gracefullytruthful.com

Anna in Waiting

Liz Carter

THEY call me a prophetess.

I sometimes wonder if I'm worthy of the name. My life hasn't been a sparkling example of God's power, because my life has been a wait.

A long wait.

Today, though, I can hear something in the distance. Something like the ringing of bells at the edges of my hearing. Something bright dancing into my vision, too. Something beckoning ...

It's so long ago, now. So long since I saw the face of my beloved husband. I can hardly summon his features in my mind, removed from me by the years. His deep brown eyes reach through time and touch me anew. Sixty years ago, it was. Sixty years since he died, left me all alone. A widow at twenty-four, a figure of pity and uselessness.

Nothing left to live for.

A broken young woman with long dark hair and eyes veiled in mourning garb, I dragged my feet through the dust-covered streets to the Temple. I wasn't even sure what I was looking for. A something. Something to lift my eyes and fling my loneliness far from me. So I went.

And I never left.

The Temple drew me in, seized my spirit and restored my soul. Exposed the hurting places deep inside and turned me inside out. There was no other place I could conceive of being. My song became that of the Psalmist, in Psalm 84:

> How lovely is your dwelling place, O LORD of hosts!
> My soul longs, yes, faints for the courts of the LORD;
> my heart and flesh sing for joy to the living God.

Even the sparrow finds a home,
and the swallow a nest for herself.

My home was near the altar of my King, and it changed me. Yet somehow, I'm still not quite there. I stand on the edge of the Holy of Holies, desperate to enter. I cannot go in, I know; but my heart is heavy with yearning. I gaze at the thick linen curtain, heavy with age and ponderous sanctitude, and wonder. What if ...?

The bells are ringing more clearly. I look up into the morning sky, a clear azure expanse, no cloud in sight, and an impression of something weaves through my mind. The holy curtain in swathes of thick darkness ... and something more. An immense rend, as if the whole fabric is being ruptured. Top to bottom.

My heart swells with a bursting joy I've never even imagined.

The image fades, but the bells still peal, a faint echo of a startling impression. The sound is something resonant. Something which tugs at my deepest place. I want to follow the sound and drench myself in it.

Through sixty long years, I fasted and I prayed. I searched for the redemptive work of my God through my waiting, catching enthralling glimpses and captivating shadows, but never seeing my waiting come to an end. In the early days, I was impatient. I was ready for God to act. My heart was bursting with passion for the Lord, and zeal for the love and mercy of God to be known throughout the land. All around me I saw hardship and struggle, the country under harsh Roman rule; and even some of my fellow Jews seemed to be so bound up in the law they forgot about love. They forgot about justice rolling like rivers, and righteousness like never-failing streams.

But I never forgot.

I fasted and I prayed, and I waited.

I gaze across the temple courts now as a commotion makes itself known. The brightness I caught the edge of earlier is stronger now, lines of shimmering light hovering somewhere on the horizon. I shield my eyes and watch the small group standing over to my left. Simeon I know well. He's one of the good ones. The most righteous man I know, and he's like me. He's been waiting for so long. He's so certain he will see the promised Messiah before he dies. His confidence has been a mainstay for me in my darker times, carrying me through. I squint through the strange brightness and move closer.

A baby. He's holding a baby. A woman and a man stand close, their faces full of puzzlement, but something else, too. There's joy there. There's a lighting up from within. I strain to catch his words. 'My eyes have seen your salvation,' he says.

My heart leaps in my chest, and the bells ring more loudly.

What could he mean?

He bends close to the woman, whispers words in her ear. I watch as her eyes fill with tears. Simeon stands back, and I look at his face.

Peace rests on him in tangible waves.

I move closer. The light is brighter now, drawing me in, enfolding me in something I have only dreamed of. Something like the yearning I've known for so long in my waiting, the desperation to be in the place my heart pines for most.

The presence of God.

The bells are ringing louder, the skies resounding in an anthem of praise, and I know.

I know.

The baby gazes up at me with dark eyes so full of innocence, and with the weight of glory. I step over to the woman, and she hands him to me. So new, so perfect.

So holy.

I give thanks to God, and know that my years of waiting are over. They culminate in this love-soaked moment, in the profound beauty of the tiny baby in my arms, who is somehow the fulfilment of all I have been longing for.

The redemption of Jerusalem.

The restoration of me.

PRAYER
Dear Jesus,
In my waiting time
May I know that you long to restore me
To touch my life with your presence.
May I yearn for the place where you are,
Step into the Holy of Holies without shame or guilt,
Because you beckon me in,
You have rent the curtain in two,
In reckless, outrageous love.
                    Amen

Liz Carter is a writer living in Shropshire with her vicar husband and two teens. She's the author of Catching Contentment *(IVP, due out at the end of 2018) and* A Tale of Beauty from Ashes, *a Bible study course based around* Beauty and the Beast.

Waiting for the Saviour

Marie Wells

I am waiting for the Saviour to come
Knocking upon my door.
I remember he came at Christmas time
He may come now once more.

I want him to know he is welcome here,
Whenever he comes to call
For though inside there is such disarray,
I know he is my all.

I am waiting for the Saviour to come
I will not hide my need.
I can sometimes go not listening at all,
Faith like a mustard seed.

The Bible tells us the Saviour will come
Mighty God, Prince of Peace.
The abode of God forever with men,
Sorrow forever to cease.

I'm waiting for the Saviour to come
Not with an empty dream,
But a promise divine of a great return
From a Lord who has already been.

Marie Wells is a full-time wife and mother, bringing up three lovely, lively children in Devon with their large dog. She has always loved writing, particularly Christian poetry and children's stories.

The Famous or Infamous Five

Pam Pointer

Bible reading: Matthew 1:1–17

HAVE you ever investigated your family tree? How many skeletons emerged from the cupboard, I wonder? What intrigues and infidelities, shocks and shenanigans, did you find? And how many had been swept under the rug in an attempt to erase them from your family history?

How fascinating it is to read the genealogy of Jesus and see, from the names mentioned, that his human ancestry consisted of a very mixed bag of people. None of the seamier side of his heritage is hidden; it's all there in the Bible for us to see, not least the mention of five women in the genealogy—each of whom could cause eyebrows to be raised.

TAMAR, whose story is in Genesis 38, was made pregnant by her father-in-law, Judah, one of the twelve sons of Jacob. Before Jacob died he declared that it was to be Judah from whom the royal line would eventually emerge. Jesus, as we know, would be the ultimate outcome. Tamar had been married, in turn, to two of Judah's sons but Judah didn't keep his promise to give her his third son in marriage—as tradition dictated. Tamar veiled herself and Judah mistook her for a prostitute and slept with her, and she gave birth to twins, one of whom, Perez, would continue the royal line.

RAHAB is the second woman to be mentioned in the genealogy. Her story is in Joshua 2 & 6. She was a prostitute whose house was built into the wall of Jericho. Joshua sent spies into the land and Rahab housed them. She'd heard about God and was prepared to stand on his side and risk her life for others. She was brave, loyal, resourceful—and a liar! When Jericho fell she was rescued, along with her family, and subsequently had a son, Boaz. She gets a mention in the Hall of Fame in Hebrews 11 as a person of faith and of friendly welcome.

RUTH is one of the best-loved love stories in the Bible. She was a widow but loyal to her mother-in-law. Famine drove them out of their home to a foreign land. Impoverished as a refugee, she found work with Boaz, the son of Rahab. Boaz was a local landowner and treated Ruth with immense respect and kindness. Reader, she married him. They had a son, Obed. Obed's son was Jesse and Jesse's youngest son was David who became king.

BATHSHEBA we read about in 2 Samuel 11. Bathsheba was married to Uriah, a soldier. She was beautiful, which spelled trouble because she was spotted by the king, David, who robbed Uriah—first by taking his wife, then by taking Uriah's life so that he could marry Bathsheba. David and Bathsheba had a son who became ill and died. Bathsheba was devastated. A repentant David comforted her and they had another son, Solomon. It was through this son that the line would be continued.

MARY is the fifth woman to be mentioned in the genealogy and she became the mother of Jesus. She was probably a young teenager, already pledged to marry Joseph. Her pregnancy—not by Joseph—caused Joseph such concern that he felt obliged to break off the betrothal. Thankfully an angel stepped into Joseph's dream and reassured him that Mary hadn't been unfaithful and that he should go ahead and marry her, as the baby had been conceived by ... the Holy Spirit!

Deceitful widow Tamar; canny prostitute Rahab; bold refugee Ruth; king's mistress Bathsheba; pregnant teenager Mary. Would you have chosen any of them to play a role in the ancestry of Jesus? Their credentials, to our judgemental human eyes, were surely not worthy of being ancestors of the Son of God! Just as well it's God who's in control and not us. How reassuring it is to know that we don't have to be perfect to be valuable to God. Indeed, we can't be perfect. Nevertheless, God loves each person and has given each a unique personality and a particular set of gifts and abilities. He calls each of his followers, whatever they're like, to be his witnesses. I am his ambassador where he's put me. You are part of his purposes, wherever he has put you. We may never know how our role is of significance in God's cosmic plan; we may never be told how our faith has encouraged someone else, how our seemingly inauspicious life may have impacted our family, our workplace, our church, our friends.

Tamar, Rahab, Ruth, Bathsheba and Mary would surely be astonished if they knew their lives would be read and talked about thousands of years after they lived! All were loved by God, used by God for his purposes and played a vital role in the human family tree of Jesus the Saviour.

Pam Pointer, writer, speaker and photographer, is the author of a dozen non-fiction and poetry books and also writes meditations, features and columns for various publications. She writes a weekly blog on her website http://pampointer.wordpress.com where details of her most recent book, Help! I'm a New Mum! *may also be found.*

Unto Us a Son is Born

Ronald Clements

And I will make of you a great nation, and I will bless you.
Genesis 12:2

THE bench was an uncomfortable old thing. Roughly hewn lengths of wood hammered together with long metal spikes, propped up on pitted slabs of the local limestone. The timber had long since weathered to grey, the spikes rusted red.

The woman who sat on the bench was, to the first glance, young. She wore a simple woollen tunic that fell to her ankles. There were no sandals on her feet. Beneath her shawl her black hair fell to the curves of her shoulders, shielding her olive skin from the sun. But when she lifted her head from the handwritten pages on her lap, there were lines and shadows in her face telling a different story.

She had lifted her head because the scuff of footsteps on the narrow dirt path to the crest of the hill where she was sitting announced the arrival of someone else. Slowly climbing towards her with the aid of a long stick was an old man. He was a curious figure, wrapped in the layers of the ancient shepherds, and wearing a *kaffiyeh*, a soft cloth headdress held in place with a length of black leather cord. As he approached she lowered her head and waited for him to pass by.

'May I rest a while?'

The woman looked up, startled that he had spoken to her. 'Yes ... of course.' She shuffled well to one side, allowing room for his robes.

'You were expecting someone else? I see it in your face.'

'Yes. My son. But please ...' The woman gestured to him to sit.

The old man lowered himself onto the bench. He leant forward a little, his knees spread wide, his hands high on the stick planted between his feet.

'Have you come far?' asked the woman.

The man ran his hand down the crudely cut notches on his stick. 'Two thousand years,' he replied.

The woman suppressed a surprised laugh, placing her hand over her mouth.

'But not without reason. I am looking for my family.'

'Your family?'

'It is not that they are lost. I am trying to find out who they are.'

The woman looked confused, but the man carried on, 'You are waiting for your son? I waited for my son. He was a long time coming. My wife, Sarah, was barren. I was as old as the oak trees we lived beneath. Some called him a miracle. We called him Isaac—' he laughs '—because we laughed.'

'Sarah? Isaac? Then you are ... Abraham?'

'Yes. How would you know?'

And then the woman did laugh, aloud, 'Because everyone knows your story. How the three strangers came to Mamre predicting Isaac's birth. How Sarah laughed. And Isaac being born. My mother told me the story. It was a miracle! See ...' She rapidly thumbed through the pages on her lap.

'Here ... Abraham was a hundred years old when his son Isaac was born to him. Sarah said, 'God has brought me laughter ...''

'So she did,' said Abraham. 'It was God, you know, who came,' he continued. 'Sitting there beneath the trees, just as I am sitting here with you. I knew it afterwards. And if God promised something, who was I to doubt it?'

'God promised me a son,' said the woman.

'The one you are waiting for?'

'Yes. He came, just as God said he would. We called him Yeshua.'

'Yeshua ... "he saves"?'

'Yes.'

Abraham took the page from her and studied it. 'Did your mother tell you the other promises that God made? One evening I wandered out under the night sky and he said my family would be like the stars; thousands upon thousands. A great nation.'

'She did,' replied the woman. 'She said all the people on earth would be blessed through you.'

'That is why I am looking for my family. I want to know if they have been a blessing as God promised. You are laughing at me?'

'No ... I am laughing because I am one of your family. One of your thousands upon thousands.'

'And the blessing? Has there been the promised blessing?' Abraham sounded anxious.

'Oh, yes,' nodded the woman. 'There has been the greatest blessing.'

Abraham sat back against the rough wood of the bench and sighed contentedly, 'It is a good thing. God has kept his promise. Who was I to doubt it?'

They said nothing for a while, until Abraham turned to the woman as though a new thought had struck him.

'What is your name, my daughter?'

'Mary.'

'And what do you know of this blessing?'

Mary shuffled through her bundle of pages again. 'Look! The words of one of our great prophets. "You"—that's God—"have enlarged the nation and increased their joy ... For to us a child is born, to us a son is given ... He will reign with justice and righteousness forever." This child is my son, Yeshua, promised by God; the Son of God, who has lived among us, and who brings life, healing and peace for all nations, if people follow him.'

'And now you are waiting for him again?'

'When he left, he said he was going to heaven. He promised to return. And if the Son of God promised something, who am I to doubt him?'

'I would like to meet this special son of yours,' said Abraham. 'May I wait with you?'

'Of course,' said Mary. 'Perhaps I can tell you my story?'

And then she began to sing and her words drifted down the valley and across the generations for two thousand years.

'My soul glorifies the Lord and my spirit rejoices in God my Saviour, for he has been mindful of the humble state of his servant. He has helped his servant Israel, remembering to be merciful to Abraham and his descendants forever, just as he promised our ancestors …'

Ronald Clements is a full-time freelance writer. His books include Lives from a Black Tin Box *and* In Japan the Crickets Cry, *missionary biographies set in Africa and Asia. He has written for feature films and written/ directed TV documentaries, as well as produced Christian apologetic and resource material. www.ronaldclements.com*

Destination Earth

Jan Richardson

Did you know about the gruelling journey
about the lack of accommodation
about the bitter cold of the cave?

Did you predict, when you stepped into time
that you would slip into a hay-lined trough
cry out in bloodied disbelief?

Did you wait for the shepherds,
steeped in wonder,
cradling their first-born lambs
sacrifice for sacred sacrifice?

And what about that brightest ever star?
Did you design it there in the void before time
to guide those rich magi, dusty with desert,
to deliver their unforgettable gifts?

Did you plan that in the one moment
when heaven brushed earth
angels would spill singing,
dancing right down to the hillside
where the Bethlehem sheep grazed?

And did you always know that the Christ child's
light would be born over and over
into the empty celebrations
into the places of hope?

Jan Richardson is a retired English and Special Needs teacher from Wendover, Buckinghamshire. She is a member of Wendover Free Church.

Fearfully and Wonderfully Made

Ruth M Bancewicz

My frame was not hidden from you
when I was made in secret,
intricately woven in the depths of the earth.
Your eyes saw my unformed substance;
in your book were written, every one of them,
the days that were formed for me,
when as yet there was none of them.

Psalm 139:15–16

YOU began life as a single cell—a fertilised egg with mother and father's DNA mingled together in a unique combination. This miniscule blob was all of you for a few hours, until it began to divide: 2 cells, 4, 8, 16, a ball, a hollow ball, and then something more complex. You were still tiny, but developing a nervous system, a head, a body, arms and legs. By that point your mother would be only too aware she was expecting a baby—the physical symptoms would have been hard to ignore. Each pregnancy is unique. Different parents, circumstances, extended family and wider social and cultural settings mean that no two individuals— even twins—turn out exactly the same. But we all have the same fragile start, both physically and in a sense socially too, because every family has its own special set of baggage.

In the run-up to Christmas I have often thought about Jesus' birth—his mother struggling through labour in an unfamiliar place, his undignified entry to the world, his first breath, first cry, and everything else it means to be a tiny baby. Until recently I hadn't really thought much about Jesus being an embryo.

Somehow, I find that thought even more shocking than his birth. How could God, who made the universe, have become something so completely and utterly vulnerable? Maybe in the past, when the development of a child happened in 'secret', with no imaging technology and no IVF, it was possible just to let that part of the Christmas story go untold.

Today, when we see images of a developing child, or even embryos outside the womb, it is harder to ignore the process of Jesus developing into a baby. The incarnation meant that God's son went through all the stages in the diagram in my developmental biology textbook: 'zygote', 'morula', 'blastocyst', implantation, and so on. One of the things that fills me with wonder is the formation of fingers. Our hands started out shaped like paddles. Chemical signals radiated out across the future hand, telling each cell what kind of tissue it should become: skin, cartilage, bone, muscle, and so on. The identity of each finger is determined by signals from the flaps of webbed skin between, which are eventually broken down. Pictures of developing mouse embryos show tiny digits emerging and taking on more and more detail, like a picture coming into focus.

The development of an embryo is a little like a cross between origami and stone carving. The cells multiply rapidly to form whole sheets which fold in, out, and under each other to make the embryo. So life doesn't unfold, as some book titles proclaim, it folds up. Some chiselling away is also needed, because the gut, gaps between the fingers, and other spaces need to open up to allow movement and flow. A baby only needs about one third of the nerve cells it produces during prenatal development, for example. At a cellular level, a huge amount of energy goes into producing a healthy child.

The Gospel of John begins, 'In the beginning was the Word, and the Word was with God, and the Word was God. He was in the beginning with God. All things were made through him, and without him was not any thing made that was made. In him was life, and the life was the light of men.' Jesus the Messiah, the

Word, was there in the beginning, and all life owes its existence to him. But instead of remaining aloof, content to be the one to whom all life owes its existence, he chose to become one of us. I think the incarnation lends enormous dignity to living things. The Son of God shared the same kind of DNA as every other organism on the planet. He took on a genome, and became a single cell that went through the highly complex dance of multiplying and developing into a person. Since the incarnation, we are no longer separated from God by our organic nature. Being made of material stuff is not necessarily a downside when it comes to connecting with God because he knows what it feels like to have a body, to feel hungry and thirsty, pain and pleasure, dark and light.

So as we remember the journey of Jesus' incarnation at Christmas time, we can also remember the nine months that went before his birth: Mary's sickness as the embryo took root in her womb, growing to the size of a peanut, a curled finger, then a fist. As God's Son grew, Mary's body changed. He kicked, she needed to eat more so he could grow strong, and her movements became more and more weighed down by the baby inside her. Every single person's start in life is given special status because God took exactly the same path into the world. Every life is precious.

In Psalm 139, the writer is meditating on God's intimate knowledge of him, which began when he was an embryo. There is nothing God doesn't know about him, and no way to get away from that knowledge. The incarnation means that God's intimacy with us now extends even further. He has become one of us, lived alongside us, and shared our very fragile material nature. It's hard to get my head around that thought. To use the Psalmist's words, 'Such knowledge is too wonderful for me; it is high; I cannot attain it.'

Dr Ruth M Bancewicz is based at The Faraday Institute for Science and Religion, where her role is to help churches focus on the positive interaction between science and faith. After studying genetics at Aberdeen and Edinburgh Universities, she worked for the UK-based professional group Christians in Science. She has written several books, and blogs at scienceandbelief.org.

Advent Adventure

Shirley Moore

My dictionary tells me Advent and adventure
are both from Old French words, and mean
'come', 'arrival' and 'about to happen'.

The words are meaningless,
as what is about to happen
is twenty something worrying days.

Twenty something days remembering
the joyful anticipation of
Christmas past.

Twenty something days of struggling,
planning, shopping, wrapping
Christmas presents.

Twenty something days wondering
if there will be
Christmas yet to come?

Wondering? Wonder! Is that the word
hidden under mounds of
Christmas tinsel?

Wonder of Mary, meeting an angel.
Wonder of Elizabeth's baby, leaping in her womb.
Wonder of Joseph, convinced by a dream.
Wonder of shepherds, under a sky of angels.

Wonder of Wise Men, following a star.
Wonder of all who saw that special child.

If I can hold on to that wonder
Christmas will come.
I will sense its arrival.
This is what is about to happen
on my Advent Adventure.

Shirley Moore lives in Sheffield and has been writing poems and stories for most of her long life. She says that this poem was written because she often struggles to balance her Christian life with the pressures of the world.

Emmanuel's Love

'The Sun of righteousness will rise with healing in his wings'

Caroline Gill

Open my eyes to Emmanuel's love,
love in the form of an infant King;
King in a manger exalted in song,
song of the angels on high.

Stir up my soul with a gift of great joy,
joy overflowing for Christ has come;
come from the Father to shine as the light,
light for all people on earth.

Grant by your Spirit a blessing of peace,
peace from the Prince who was born to die;
die for my sins, giving pardon and grace,
grace to declare the Good News.

Shore up my life with a promise of hope,
hope I receive from my Saviour's hands;
hands that were nailed to a scaffold of wood,
wood that was Calvary's cross.

Thank you, Lord Jesus, for bountiful love,
love from my risen, ascended King.
King of my heart, Sun of righteousness, come;
come, in all majesty, come.

Caroline Gill led the ACW-affiliated Swansea Ready Writers group with her husband, David Gill, between 2002 and 2007. Caroline's website is www.carolinegillpoetry.com, and her 2012 poetry chapbook, The Holy Place, *co-authored with John Dotson, was published by The Seventh Quarry (Wales), in conjunction with Cross-Cultural Communications (New York).*

The Nativity

Imagining the Incarnation

New Parents and Angels

May it Be

Lucy Mills

may it be, she said,
as her world juddered,
as the future shifted
before her eyes;
may it be, she said,
as her life became
something more extraordinary
than before

may it be, she said,
as faith became everything—
the usual safety nets
of reputation
and human approval
stripped away

may it be, she said,
with a courage
that would make her
world famous
in the end

may it be.

❀

Lucy Mills is a writer, editor and speaker. She's authored two books:
Forgetful Heart *and* Undivided Heart. *Find out more about her at*
www.lucy-mills.com

A Mother's Story

Heather Johnston

I SIT by the window looking up at the stars. My mind is in a whirl and I can't sleep. Mary has been quiet and preoccupied for the last two weeks but I waited, knowing that she would tell me in her own good time, and today she did. We had set the bread to rise and were resting outside in the sun when she spoke.

'Mother, I don't know how to tell you this but … I'm going to have a baby—' she held up her hand as I started to speak. 'It's not how you think, so please let me finish. I had a visit from an angel and he told me I have been chosen to be the mother of God's Son. The Holy Spirit will come upon me and I will conceive through him. He also said that the child of Elizabeth our kinswoman, who is pregnant in her old age, is part of God's plan too. I said to the angel, "I am God's servant and will do whatever is needed of me." Please believe me. You know I have always been a devout God-fearing girl and I would never bring disgrace on myself and my family.'

She put her hand in mine, and after a few minutes I spoke.

'I'm finding it hard to take this in, Mary; yet I know you've never lied to us or deceived us. But … What about Joseph? Have you told him?'

'That's the wonderful thing! When I first told him, he said he'd end our engagement quietly, but then he had a dream and the angel appeared to him, telling him what he'd told me and saying that our marriage must go ahead. Our son is to be called Jesus and he will save our people from sin. So he must be the promised Messiah. Our marriage will go ahead as planned but…' she hesitated and blushed, 'we will not sleep as man and wife until after the baby is born. Please, Mother, please say you understand and trust me to do God's will.'

I gathered her in my arms. 'Of course I trust you, my dear child, and I'll support you and Joseph through all this.'

She sighed. 'Thank you, Mother, but what about Father?'

'Leave him to me. Say nothing and I'll find the right time to tell him. Come on—I think that bread will be risen by now.'

Here I am sitting by the window and I still haven't found the right time to tell him. Don't get me wrong, Joachim is a good man and a believer, but he keeps his belief to himself—he doesn't show emotion, although I know he adores his 'little girl' as he still calls her. So how do I tell him? I know what one of his reactions will be: 'This is a small town! There'll be tittle-tattle, finger-pointing, how will we cope with that?' I've thought of this too and a plan is forming that when Mary starts to show she can go and stay with Elizabeth for a while.

As I sit here, the sun starts to appear over the horizon. The sky is streaked with red, yellow and gold, and I remember Mary's words to the angel: 'I am God's servant and will do whatever is needed of me.' I know now that the same applies to me, and God will show me the right time and words.

I creep back to our mattress and lie down beside a snoring Joachim. I smile as something I had not thought of before comes into my mind. 'I'm going to be a grandmother and you, my dear Joachim, are going to be a grandfather. All will be well.'

Heather Johnston is retired and living in Coldingham, Scottish Borders, where she enjoys reading, writing, walking beside the sea, involvement in the life of Coldingham Priory and singing in a Community Choir. She has written for several Christian anthologies and Together *and* Roots *magazines, and self-published two poetry collections.*

United Only by a Star

Margaret Gee

THE woman leant heavily against the doorpost of her home as she pulled her robe around her trembling body. She needed some warmth, without a doubt, but she also longed for a shred of comfort for the anguish in her heart.

The rest of her family were asleep inside, and she did not want to wake them. She had been struggling to fight back the tears all day, and it was such hard, hard work. How could she explain the grief which followed her wherever she went? How could she rip her loyalty in two and share it equally? She felt torn apart and did not know how to face another day.

Now that she was alone, however, she had something else to think about. She had strange pains low down in her stomach which were getting stronger by the hour. She remembered a time when her sister was giving birth and she could almost feel the labour pains herself. It was so strange but she recognised that same feeling now, just as when she had given birth herself.

Mary! Was it Mary? Could it be that Mary was giving birth right now? A sob came from deep within her and now the tears began to flow. Shuddering, body-shaking sobs that brought her to her knees. She did not know how long it was before the tears eased and she turned to look into the night sky. It was clear and bright, and even through her wet eyes she could make out the stars.

One seemed to shine more brightly than most that night and the memories tumbled over themselves as she thought back over the past year. She would never forget the moment when Mary told them that an angel had come to visit her. What! Of all the stories that teenagers could make up, that surely had to be the most outrageous.

Her husband had plans for Mary to marry one of the local boys. He was a good man, was Joseph, and was working hard at his trade. He certainly had eyes for Mary but she was just lost in a faraway world where no one could seem to reach her.

She remembered so clearly when Mary had told her that she planned to go and visit her cousin Elizabeth. She had it all worked out. There was a determination about this girl of theirs which had taken them by surprise. Mary had always been so willing to please them and do what she could to support the family in these hard times. But since the story about 'the angel' something had come over her. They just could not understand it.

She promised that she would come back and they had no choice but to let her go. She would remember every move of Mary's head, every step she took as she left the village that day. She wondered if other mothers felt as she did when their daughters left home.

Her heart had ached for her then, wondering if she got to Elizabeth's village and how she was getting on. There was no means of knowing and she simply had to get through the days as best she could.

It helped to be busy, but then the act of survival always made life busy. From sunrise to sunset there was always something to be done.

Yes! She remembered all those moments, but none more so than the day when Mary reappeared on a donkey cart, having come home with some neighbours. As the village children called Mary's name she had rushed out to meet her, but stopped suddenly. Everyone had stopped. Everyone stared. Mary was pregnant. It was unmistakable.

She remembered how angry Mary's father had been. She could see the pain in Joseph's eyes even now. Her own heart had felt ripped to pieces.

Mary had remained adamant that she had not been with anyone. No! She had *not* been raped by one of the soldiers. She had *not* been unfaithful. The angel had told her ...

In the days that followed her own loyalty was pulled so hard in both directions. She had to be faithful to her husband and he was still so angry. She had to bear the shame of the neighbours, and they were so unforgiving. But she was a mother and her daughter was hurting. This Mary of hers (yes, despite everything, Mary was still her daughter) was carrying a message so huge, even bigger than the swelling in her stomach.

She remembered the teaching that had been handed down from one generation to another. It was the message of a Messiah who would come to save His people. She remembered something about a star.

She was grateful that Joseph had not been the one to throw a stone at Mary, nor allowed others to do it either. She admired the way he had said he would stick with her. She remembered when the summons came for everyone to take part in a census and each had to return to the town of their birth. How could she ever forget?

The tears fell again now as she recalled the pain of watching Mary and Joseph leave the village under the stony stares of the neighbours, knowing deep within her heart that she would probably never see her daughter again. And now as she clutched her stomach and looked at that bright shining star, she breathed a prayer that Adonai would take care of them. Somehow, she now knew that what Mary had told them was true, and that she had been called to bear this special child.

When history is in the making do we really know? Mary's mother could only know in part. As families gather this Christmas time we take a moment to honour those extended family members and friends who share 'the call' of someone they love, perhaps also only knowing in part and missing them so much.

Margaret Gee has a passion that people would know of the welcome awaiting them at The King's Table *and her latest book explores this through the tragic story of Mephibosheth. Details of this, and her other books can be found at www.unfoldingpromises.com*

Would You Believe It!

Joanna Ray

NOBODY could believe it! Stories had been flying round the whole area for weeks. Old Elizabeth had claimed she'd actually given birth to a baby boy! (Of course, everyone knew that she and Zachariah couldn't have children at their late age.) Poor Zachariah had been struck dumb and now there were rumours that the young relation staying with them was also expecting a baby—and she wasn't even married!

'*Not* the sort of goings on I would expect to hear from a *priest's* family!' whispered one woman as she drew water from the village well.

'Certainly not!' agreed her friend. '*Especially* not one serving in the Temple of the Lord!'

'Would you believe it? It's a scandal!' hissed another.

Of course, Elizabeth and her husband had soon found out who their friends were. Some had rejoiced at their news, but when Elizabeth called a party to circumcise and name the baby the whole village turned up.

'Well! I'm sure you're all dying to hear our news,' Elizabeth began, as an immediate hush fell on the whole gathering. 'As you know,' she continued, her head held high, 'nine months ago my husband had the great honour of being chosen to enter the holiest place in Jerusalem's Temple. Such a day comes to very few men and I was proud of him. What happened there, however, is something of a mystery as, er, unfortunately, he has become dumb.'

Someone tutted, disapprovingly, another cleared his throat, rather too noisily.

'However,' Elizabeth continued, looking them straight in the eye, 'my husband has written everything down! My young cousin

Mary, who's been a wonderful help to me, will now *read* you his story.'

All eyes became fixed on Mary.

A little nervously, the girl opened Zachariah's scroll, and started reading in a clear, quiet voice:

'Dear friends, this year I, Zachariah, Priest of the Order of Abijah, was chosen to enter the Temple of the Lord, to carry incense into the very presence of the Lord, who dwells in the Holy of Holies. I can't begin to tell you what that moment meant to me. Hundreds of worshippers gathered outside, waiting and praying. However, what happened there simply paralysed me with fear! I saw—in fact I was dazzled by—a visitation from the Archangel Gabriel!'

Some guests gasped. Others muttered under their breath.

Unsteadily, Mary continued reading. 'Perhaps what happened next should not have shaken me so much, but the Archangel began telling me extraordinary things! He said we *would* have a son after all—that our newborn would be great in God's sight. Indeed, he said that our son would turn unbelievers to God—that he would be sent to prepare people for the coming of our longed-for Messiah himself!'

At this point no one moved.

Mary continued, 'Well, I'm almost too ashamed to describe what happened next. Not only did I not believe it, I started arguing with the Archangel Gabriel! I asked him what sort of proof he had—because of our extreme old age you understand.'

Some guests murmured sympathetically.

Mary's reading grew stronger. 'In a voice that seemed to me like thunder the Archangel replied, "I am Gabriel who stands before God, sent to bring you this glorious news, but you only speak of unbelief! You will now be silent, unable to speak. These things *will* come to pass!"'

Mary sat down. No one spoke.

Elizabeth was the first to recover her composure.

'Well!' she said, tossing her head, 'now we'll get on with what we've come for: the naming of our wonderful, miracle baby! He is to be named John.'

Then, everyone found their voices! '*John?*' They choused, in shocked disapproval. 'Elizabeth! His name should be Zachariah!'

In the confusion Zachariah's oldest friend, Alpheus, decided that it was time for him to bring a little order into the situation. Struggling to his feet and rapping his staff on the floor he announced, with exaggerated condescension, 'Elizabeth, we do appreciate that ... er ... after all your ... er ... "excitement" and due to your splendidly advanced years, things can become a tiny bit confused. Of course you *meant* that your first-born must be called Zachariah, after his saintly father. That, as you will know, is our revered custom.'

Elizabeth raised her eyebrows. 'His name is definitely John!' she replied firmly and with some dignity.

The hubbub continued—this time in whispers. 'Poor Zechariah! Isn't he suffering enough?'

'That's an insult to his family line!'

'Her age is probably affecting her mind.'

Alpheus waved his stick for attention. 'You *must* know Elizabeth that there has never ever been *anyone* in Zachariah's line called John!'

'That's right!' choused the guests.

'*So!* We will now consult Zachariah himself.' finished Alpheus, waving his hand triumphantly towards Zachariah.

But Zachariah was already scribbling frantically on his slate, mouthing his letters as he went, 'H-i-s ... n-a-m-e ... i-s' ... but, before he'd finished, he spluttered out '*John!*' Then louder, 'His name is John. The Archangel Gabriel said so! So who am I to argue?'

There was a long pause. Suddenly someone cheered.

'He can speak!' shouted another.

Then, everyone joined in. All the men wanted to congratulate Zachariah and all the women wanted to hold the baby. John's naming party was the talk of the area for months to come.

Indeed, once Zachariah had found his tongue again there was no stopping him!

Mary alone was silent. She was trying to fathom the full implications of her own message from the same Archangel. She imagined its repercussions on her life and the world she knew. She sensed something amazing was happening, even in the heavens, something that could totally revolutionise the world. It was as if God Himself stood on the threshold of Glory, ready to break into the earth.

Joanna Ray trained at the Central School of Speech and Drama and St Michael's House Theological College, Oxford. After working in Nigeria, she returned to England, completed the BBC TV Director/Producer training and worked in TV for 20 years. Now retired she enjoys writing and photographic art.

Magnificat

Philippa Linton

Luke 1:39–55

E LISHEVA!'
My voice echoes through the house. I'm panting from
the heat and the effort of climbing the small hill. I set down my
bag of clothes, steady myself against the doorpost.

'Maryam! Oh, you blessed girl!'

Here is dear Elisheva coming towards me, her face alight, her
hands spread out in welcome.

She strokes my cheek, gazes into my eyes. Her look is deep,
as if searching out my soul. Then she takes my hand and places
it on the swollen mound of her tummy. I stare down. My own
bump is barely showing—if you didn't know, you would only
think I had become a little bit fat. My beloved parents seem to
have guessed the truth—and, oh, how the worry in their eyes
gives me sorrow—but nobody else could know. As for Elisheva,
here she is in her sixth decade, with her full womb under my
hand like an oven warm with bread, packed with secrets.

'Feel that, lass,' she says, pressing my fingers against her. 'He
kicked, a few seconds ago. When he heard you greet me, the child
leapt within me.'

My hand presses more firmly. Then I feel it!—the baby
within her kicks. We stare at each other, then break into laughter.
Elisheva ululates.

'What a miracle, what a day,' she says. 'The mother of my
Lord has come to my home ...' She puts her arm around
me. 'Come and eat. Come and rest. We have so much to talk
about.'

We sit together in the open door, gazing out over the quiet

hills and the little town nestling below. Zechariah and Elisheva's house perches on top of an incline, against the rocky face of a cliff, set some way apart from the other houses.

I am relaxed and at ease after a simple and delicious meal, and my feet are bathed. The veil on my head protects me from the heat of the sun, although it is not fierce any longer—the evening is not far off. The sunshine is very bright and gold on the smooth hills.

Elisheva keeps looking at me. Her eyes are dark, kind and wise. I return her glance as fully as I can. I have nothing to hide, because I know I am safe with her.

'Behold us two,' she says. 'You are so young, and I am so old. Yet both of us are mothers-to-be!'

'How did you know about my baby, Elisheva?'

She shrugs and spreads her hands wide again. 'Ruach Elohim.'

A strange reply, but I understand what she means. Ruach, the voice and spirit of God himself. Surely the wife of the high priest would be able to hear the voice of YHWH clearly. But then, I too have heard YHWH, seen his angel. It's hard for me to talk about. But it's good to be here with her. I know now that she understands everything.

'What an honour,' says Elisheva, 'what a blessing, that I should be sitting here with the mother of my Lord beside me.'

She pats her belly. 'He knows,' she says, 'the child within me knows who it is you carry within you. That's why he leapt.'

I am silent. These things are all so big in my mind. I have always known who my secret child is, but the knowing of it is a precious gem to be shared with only a few.

Elisheva seems to read my thoughts. Her smile is soft in the golden light. 'How did *you* find out about your baby?' she says gently.

'Gavriel,' I say. 'The angel's name was Gavriel. He *was* an angel. I know he was. He told me so.'

'*Gavriel!*' she whispers. 'Ah, Maryam … that is the same angel who came to my husband and told him about our sweet child.'

'I have heard about this angel before, Elisheva. He appears in stories in the Tanakh.'

She claps her hands together. 'Yes, yes, of course. And now he has appeared to my husband, and to you, to tell us God has given us these two boys, our miracle children.'

She leans forward then, her gaze intense. 'You do realise who your son is, Maryam?'

'His name is Yeshua. Yes, I know who he is.'

'God delivers,' she breathes.

'God saves,' I reply.

'Our people!' she exclaims.

'The whole world, Elisheva.' Suddenly I stand to my feet. 'My son will save the whole world.'

I can feel it then, the joy bubbling up within me like a spring, like a fountain. I raise my arms to the hills, to the sun beginning to slide down the sky. The world is bathed in amber light. I begin to hum, to chant.

'My soul praises YHWH, oh, how my spirit praises him …'

Elisheva beside me begins to chant too, following my words.

'I am poor and lowly, yet you, my God, have blessed me …
all the generations to follow will call me blessed …
for you are mighty and holy and have done great things for
     me, yes, you have …
you show your mercy to all those who reverence your
     name,
to each generation, so many generations …
you have shown strength with your arm,
you scatter the proud and you raise up the humble,
you have filled up the hungry with good things,
the proud and the rich will be left with nothing,
you have helped your servant Israel,
because you remember your promises to our fathers and
     our mothers,
to Avraham, to Sarah, and to all of us …'

The words rise within me, the sacred writings which my parents taught me and which I memorised, but they are also my own words and they come from the deepest part of me, from within my heart and soul, and Elisheva sings along with me, we sing and sway together in the light of the setting sun.

Philippa Linton is a licensed lay minister in her local Anglican church and also works full-time for the United Reformed Church in London. She likes art, literature, films and retreats.

Joseph's Decision

Magpie

MY mind was reeling. Mary pregnant by the Holy Spirit, and not by another man? She'll give birth to a son who will save his people from their sins? What sort of dream was that? Was I running a temperature? I went up to the olive grove to clear my head, but it stayed muddled. I couldn't concentrate on anything in my workshop either and, in the end, I went and sat in the new bedroom, under the beams I had spent so many hours carving. I'd decorated them with leaves, grapes and pomegranates; of course I chose pomegranates to symbolise fertility but this thing about the Holy Spirit making Mary pregnant—that was fertility beyond anything I'd ever imagined.

I got to thinking about wood and trees, how something grows up from the ground. You can't see the seed and yet the shoot comes up and soon you can tell if it's wheat or a vine or something else. Even the oldest olive trees started like that: tiny things in the dark that somehow grow. And the trunk of a tree doesn't look like much, it doesn't even look alive, but it's got life flowing through it. Somehow the invisible connection of the roots and the soil makes visible things pop out the other end; leaves and flowers and fruit. I got to thinking that maybe that's what the Holy Spirit is like, like sap that flows through us. The Spirit flowed through the prophets and words popped out of their mouths. Music bubbled out of the depths of David's soul. Things happen when the Holy Spirit connects you to God. Could it be true that the Holy Spirit flowed through Mary and what popped out, or at least what popped into being in the depths of her body, was not a message or a song but a whole new life—a baby, a person?

Of course, God brings all life into the world, and he can plant things in the most barren land as he did when he gave Isaac to Sarah, Samuel to Hannah, and even baby John to Mary's cousin Elizabeth. But all those women were married; it was human seed that was blessed. This would be different. This would be something out of nothing. And yet, aren't we told that in the beginning there was nothing, and then God spoke and things— life—came into being? And, in the desert, didn't God say he would provide bread and meat, and those very things appeared every day for forty years? Actually, I'm not sure how regular the quail was, but the manna appeared out of nowhere every day except Sabbath, throughout that time. The 'bread' of God's word literally became bread—became a thing that got eaten.

It was all mind-boggling, and it seemed impossible that it would have anything to do with me. Yet the person in my dream had known my name, had known Mary's name, and they had spoken with such authority.

After a while, I realised I had two options. I could ignore the dream, which was—after all—just a dream, and live in a world where Mary had cheated on me and we would never have a life together. In that scenario, if the Holy Spirit really was doing something, I'd never know, never be a part of it. Or, I could believe what I'd heard and live in a world where the Holy Spirit can create a child with no seed, and someone can save people from sin. And if it wasn't true, I'd be bringing up another man's child as my own. Could I live with that? I realised that's what my mum would assume: that I was doing the decent thing and taking an undeserving woman under my wing. In fact this was a third option, to assume that Mary had been unfaithful but marry her anyway. That would give me the moral high ground, which sounds good, but in reality would probably be hideous. Would I be able to resist forever making her pay for her betrayal? Would she be able to stop trying to make up for it? But then if there had been no betrayal she wouldn't try to make up for it—unless I made her feel she had to … Good grief, what a mess! If only I could talk to her.

Well, that wasn't going to happen before a wedding ceremony—her parents would see me as the guilty party and I'd never get near her for a private conversation. I had to decide what I believed by myself. Either Mary had turned her back on me and been with another man, or the Holy Spirit had miraculously made her pregnant. I know it sounds like foolish desperation, but the miracle seemed truer to me than the alternative. Somehow it made everything point in the same direction, like the grain in wood. I couldn't think about it anymore at that point anyway and went to eat something, got on with the day.

It was when I woke up the next morning that I knew I was going to marry Mary. I tried to explain things to my mum, but she didn't really get it. I prayed for the strength to hold onto that message of hope no matter what others thought. I didn't want to end up treating Mary, or the baby, with bitterness.

I took a deep breath and went to ask my cousin to come with me to see Mary's dad. I was backing the Holy Spirit version of reality.

Magpie lives in London and is doing well in the racking-up-unfinished-projects competition of life. She blogs sporadically about culture, identity and theology at mishkidindiscovery.wordpress.com.

Nativity (for Paddy)

Liz Manning

WHO am I? Oh, no one you notice much. I'm just the one at the back keeping my eye on things, making sure everything's ok, making sure *they're* ok, that my family is safe and sound and undisturbed.

Undisturbed? Huh! Chance'd be a fine thing! The visitors we've had recently, all sorts I can tell you, and at all times of day and night too. And the racket they and what they brought with them made! But it's amazing what a baby can sleep through. And I've done my bit to make sure the visits weren't too long or too tiring for my girl.

Been through a lot, she has, enough to wear anyone out, let alone in her condition. All sorts of gossip and badmouthing she's had to put up with. And then the paperwork to fill in, and not simple stuff you can just sort out at your local civic centre, oh no; we've had to travel miles to file it in the right place. Not that I minded, but she shouldn't have been travelling, not in her condition, not so close to her due date. She should have been at home with her mum, not in some strange town where we knew no one.

And then finding somewhere to stay once we got here—what a nightmare! I lost count of how many places we tried, how many doors I knocked on. But it's the wrong time of year to find a room when you haven't booked in advance. In the end, I was grateful even for this old dump that someone took pity and cleared out for us. At least we could sit down and rest.

Not the kind of place you'd choose to give birth in though, but better than the streets and at least things were straightforward in that department, which was a good job as it's really women's work assisting with all that. I did my best and, like

I said, no complications to worry about, thank goodness.

Amazing thing, seeing your wife give birth. I thought I might feel differently, a bit detached maybe, seeing as the baby's not, you know, not technically mine. But when it happened, I was just so relieved she was ok, that I hadn't lost her, cos you hear awful stories about some births. And when I saw him for the first time ... well, words just aren't big enough. It was love at first sight, just like with his mother. And he is the image of her so that probably helped too.

Some of you will look at pictures of us and see that I'm always there. But you won't focus on me. You'll look at the baby, and his mother; they're the natural centre of attention. And then you'll see the visitors—because, to be honest, they do look a bit strange, a bit out of place, not what you'd expect to see in a family snap. You won't notice me beyond registering my presence. But that's ok. I don't mind. You see, ever since the beginning when I agreed to take this on, I knew that my life's work would be to take care of her so that she could take care of him. I have such an important job to do.

Husband, sons, Boys' Brigade, Jesus—much of the encouragement, inspiration and distraction for Liz Manning's writing comes from her menfolk. She blogs regularly at thestufflifeismadeofblog.wordpress.com

Welcome, Little King

Caroline Greville

FIVE days ago she was in Nazareth, bags and baskets packed
for the journey, saying those lingering farewells. Her mother
clung to her and asked one last time if it was really safe for her
to travel. Joseph could do it alone, she'd reminded her; but no,
he was faithful and kind and she wanted to be by his side. Dear
Joseph. The way he looked at her and smiled—such commitment
in his face, such depth of love. God really knew what he was
doing in choosing him, though she wondered if *she* was up to the
task herself. Why exactly had she 'found favour' with God, as the
angel had said?

It really hadn't been easy though. Joseph had told her his fears
when they were alone together, that the neighbours couldn't be
trusted, especially with him out of the way. He'd protected her
so well and tried to shield her from the unkind comments, but
she knew what they said about her: 'Damaged goods', 'Harlot',
and, the worst one of all, 'Stone-worthy. He should stone her;
why didn't he?' Why did they think she couldn't hear them, or
spot the hands in front of their mouths as they whispered? She
saw the looks they gave her when she walked on by. She'd found
there was nothing she could do but keep her head down and
pass quickly. What kept her strong was the knowledge it would
change—she knew, even then, that the shame would all be gone
when this little one was born … To have him in their midst, the
most awesome thing. What her people had dreamt of for so long.
And now here he was. Incredible. Praise God, the King of Kings.
His tender mercies would know no end, and it started right here,
with this precious little one in her lap.

Five days … How much had changed since then. She dipped
her fingers in the shallow dish of olive oil beside her and ran

them over the baby's smooth skin, massaged the oil into his dark strong hair, over his cheeks and his little nose with the gentlest of touch. Did he look like her? It was hard to tell so early on, but she wondered if there would be any likeness at all. He certainly wouldn't look like Joseph, but he had the purest, deepest love of all and would be the best earthly dad she could imagine. She picked up one of the baby's small hands and felt it wrap around her finger. He held on with all of his little might. What a beautiful boy he was and how she loved him already! What an incredible gift! Her heart felt so full of love for him that she could even feel it beating; she felt more alive than ever before. What purpose he had given her, what hope! How wonderful God was, that he should have dreamt this up and thought of *her*.

She wiped the tears from her face that had started to fall onto the baby, and felt Joseph lay his big strong arm across her shoulders. He swept the remaining tear from her face. 'It's going to be all right, you know,' he said. 'We've got this far, and one fine day we'll take him home, show the family. You need to get some rest now, you must be so tired.'

'I could stay here forever, just us three,' she said as she rubbed the oil over the baby's legs and feet, her fingers lingering on his tiny toes. 'I'm in no hurry to go back anyway—it won't be easy, the gossip won't stop.' She paused. 'Can you pass me those strips of cloth?'

'One day at a time,' said Joseph, handing them to her. 'I wanted to provide you with some place better than this, but we'll find a proper room soon.'

'I'm comfy here,' she said. 'And look how settled he is.' They gazed at the baby, transfixed by him. She tenderly wrapped him in the swaddling bands then kissed him on the forehead. Joseph arranged some straw in the feeding trough next to where he was sitting, then rose, took him in his arms and placed him inside, very slowly though so as not to wake him.

There was the noise of a stampede outside and raucous shouts, the heavy feet of young men racing down the track.

'I'll go and see what's happening,' he said. But, as he spoke, there was a gentle tap on the old wooden door.

'Hello!' came a voice. 'We're looking for a baby.'

Joseph opened the door wide and it creaked a greeting. There stood an old wizened shepherd and, on catching sight of mother and child, he stepped back and bowed his head. 'We saw some angels out in the fields; they invited us down, *us*,' he said, looking at his old woollen tunic and brushing off the debris from the field. A cluster of shepherd faces joined him at the door.

'Come in,' said Joseph. 'All of you.'

'He's the Saviour of the world,' said the old shepherd. 'It's the Lord, he's here and the angels chose to tell *us*.' He shook his head in wonderment and, in a moment of boldness, went right up to the manger and knelt before him. 'Welcome, little king,' he said, and shook his head again.

A young, vital shepherd put a hand on his shoulder and knelt down beside him, and the others followed.

'Those angels, what did they say to you?' asked Joseph, sitting down again.

'It was just one who spoke, but soon there was a great crowd of them, singing their praises to God. I'm surprised you didn't hear them from here.' The old shepherd told them what the angel had said and the hearts of all were warmed.

'What've you done with your sheep?' asked Joseph, and they laughed together.

'Come on, lads, we'd better go. Pleased to meet you, little king.'

Caroline Greville teaches Creative Writing and Creative Non-Fiction for Christ Church University, Canterbury and Kent Adult Education. She has written Badger Clan, *a nature memoir currently out on submission with publishers. Her nature writing is also to be found in the Seasons anthologies (Elliott and Thompson for The Wildlife Trusts). She has written devotions for* The Upper Room Bible notes.

Newborn Dreams

Philip S Davies

THE stable door creaked open just enough for the man to emerge into the inn's darkened courtyard. He closed the door gently behind him.

His clothing was poor. He looked like a craftsman, with hands strong, but rough. With utmost tenderness, he cradled a bundle of cloths in his arms. He wandered out to the narrow street, and then stopped to look at the stars glimmering brightly overhead. He let out a deep breath, and it condensed before him in the cool, night air. He hugged the bundle closer to his chest.

The bundle stirred. Tiny newborn fingers poked from the tangle of cloths, with a murmur of warmth and contentment. The man hummed a lullaby as he paced the baby to sleep.

When the infant settled, he sighed.

'What a night, eh?' He spoke softly—perhaps to himself, perhaps to the baby, or simply addressing the night sky.

'What a night. I don't think we got much sleep, did we? But Mary's sleeping now, Mummy's asleep. She needs the rest most of all, don't you think? And you can sleep too, while Daddy looks after you.'

He chuckled. 'Perhaps I should clarify that "Daddy looking after you" means that when you need feeding, or changing, or if you're sick or start crying your head off, I hand you straight back to Mummy. All right? Sorry about that, but I'm afraid that's the way it is. What Daddy gets to do is hold you while you're asleep and settled, and talk to you a bit.'

He set off down the deserted street towards the edge of town. 'So, yes, that's me, your Daddy. Joseph by name, but you'll call me "Daddy". And your name is Jesus. Jesus. I guess we'll get used to the name. Now I think of it, talking of "Daddy", if what they say is true, then God Himself is really your Father. God Himself. But if it's all right with you, I'll be your Daddy too. And you're here now, and healthy, and that's what's most important.'

He stopped and picked at the bundle of cloths. 'What's this you've got here? Bits of straw? I don't know. To think a son of mine should be born in a stable, and laid in a manger. There's one thing though: you've started early with the woodwork. It won't be the last manger you'll see when you start working for Joseph and Son Carpentry Shop!'

He walked on and lifted his eyes to the heavens. 'And did you hear that singing? I'm sure all Bethlehem heard it, maybe all Judea. And what singing. The most beautiful I've ever heard. Choirs of angels they said, and I can believe it. I'll remember that music for ever: "Glory to God in the highest heaven, and peace to His people on earth."'

He reached the edge of town, and looked up at the shadowy hillsides. 'What did you make of those shepherds? Not the first thing we thought about, right after the birth, in the middle of the night, to receive visitors. But they wanted to see you, didn't they? So full of wonder, so full of joy. But you have to admit, they … smelled. Perhaps I should explain: there are different sorts of people. There are skilled and trained craftsmen, such as us. Then there are shepherds. Uncouth, unkempt, and, yes, smelly. Not the sort we normally mix with. But they came, sent by angels, they said, so what could we do? Can't see why angels would appear to shepherds, though.'

He paused and regarded the bundle in his arms. 'But, of course, if what I've heard is true, then you know all of this already, don't you? It's just … at the moment … it doesn't seem that way, with you so tiny, so helpless, so fragile. Feels like it's your Daddy's job to teach you, but I don't see how that'll work out. Anyway, what did those shepherds say? "To you is born this day in the city of David a Saviour, who is Christ the Lord." So that will be you then, will it?'

Tears sprang to his eyes. 'A Saviour, Christ the Lord. I wonder.

Maybe you'll bring a bit more hope and joy to this world. Can't say as that's a bad thing.'

He looked around him, and there was silence. 'It's strange. Although in one way the world looks exactly the same as ever, somehow I know that everything's changed. And that's not just a first-time father feeling the sudden responsibility of parenthood. No, it's all about you, isn't it? You've changed the world, haven't you, simply by being born.'

He shook himself. 'But don't you worry about any of that just yet. You take your time. Don't rush to grow up too soon. Plenty of time later for being Saviour of the world. Not just yet, not just yet.'

He shivered. 'Come on. That's enough fresh air for tonight. There'll be plenty of nights for starlit walks. Let's go and see how Mummy is.'

He started back into town.

Safe in his father's arms the newborn baby slept, oblivious for now of all the sorrows and cares of the world. Before them, the first light of dawn was breaking for a new day.

Revd. Philip S. Davies is a Priest in the Church of England, and former Chair of the U.K. Association of Christian Writers. He is the author of the Destiny's Rebel *trilogy of fantasy adventure novels for young people, published by Books to Treasure.*

The Nativity

The Birth

Coming

Andrea Sarginson

A story based on the tradition that two midwives were present at
Jesus' birth

RUBE … what are you doin' knockin' me up at this time?
You must have had a job on the road in the dark. All those
potholes … and alone. An' all the stuff you're carryin'. Come in.'
'No, not so bad. I could see fine; it's right starry. And there's
too many folks still on the road for a lone woman to be in danger.
Sal … I've just had word from the inn down yonder, they sent
their lad. Can you come? They've a baby about to arrive.'
'Aye, I guessed as much from your bags. But it's busy here,
Rube. I've enough guests of my own to keep me more than
busy an' they'll need breakfast at sun-up. Can't they deal with
it themselves? Ruth's had that inn long enough to deal with
anythin'. Don't you remember a while back when them Roman
soldiers arrived an' …'
'Sal, stop prattlin', this is different. The lad said the inn's
chocker and this couple arrived, just after midnight. She was way
into labour. There was a bit of a commotion by all accounts.
They've had to put 'em in the stable with all the messed-up straw
an' animals, cos there's no rooms free.'
'Well at least it'll be warm.'
'Sal, the mother's nobbut a lass. Arrived on a donkey groanin'
she did, wi' an old man the lad says is the father. Apparently, he's
fussin' around like a mother hen; clucking about the lass and
makin' things worse. The lad looks a bit green. I guess he's seen
a few things he's a bit too young to know about. I had to leave
him with my husband an' a bottle of summat strong. Mind you,

83

that's no hardship for my Seth. Any road, Sal, can you come? It sounds bad, the baby could be stuck. An' you know how workin' together, we've had some successes.'

'How's the lass takin' it?'

'Well, that's the weird thing. According to the lad, she's in pain right enough but calm an' repeatin' again an' again, "It'll be fine, it'll be fine."'

'Well, 'appen it will be. You know how long first babies can take.'

'Yes but ...'

'I'm really busy with my own guests, Rube. This census has caused no end of problems ...'

'I know Sal but there's somethin' about this that's different. The lad was scared. Said the star that's been comin' up over the horizon is the brightest he's ever seen. It moves and tonight it's over the inn. You can see it from 'ere. Look. To tell the truth, I think he's glad to be away. He won't go back until its daylight, I'm sure. By then both he an' my husband'll be legless. Oh Sal, please come. Our midwifery skills are second to none. Though I say it myself as shouldn't.'

'Ee, Rube, if we don't say it, who will? How young is she?'

'She's nobbut a maiden—barely old enough to be a mother, very short, very thin except for her large bump. This has to be her first. It looks like it's the father's first an' all, by the way he's fussin'. The lad says he keeps wringin' his hands and sayin' "It's precious, it's *really* precious."'

'Oh Rube, I don't know. *My* guests are precious. I've put them up as a favour and they'll pay good money for good service. Will the couple pay us?'

'Sal ... I'm sorry. I don't know. I didn't think.'

'Ee ... you're a soft-un, an' no mistake.'

'I wouldn't ask you but things are not normal with this couple. I feel it. You know what my second sight is like. And I know the lad from the inn. They've sent him because he tells it as it is. There's summat up and they need us. Look ... the long and short of it is … there's a very young, small, first-time mum with an old man for a husband. The inn is heavin', largely with men. The lass has been groanin' for hours. She's had a long journey on a stinking donkey, they're in a stable with animals. The birthing bed is a pile of straw. I guess there's hardly a clean cloth left in the place. There's a strange, really bright star in the sky. No wonder the baby is reluctant to arrive. I'm goin' there, Sal, whether you come or not but … please come with me. I … I need you.'

'Aye, all right. I'll get some clean cloths; I've plenty put by. It's a one-off census so I don't suppose my guests are likely to come again anyway, so I won't have to face 'em in the future. It was just a nice opportunity to get a bit of extra cash. If they complain … so be it. If I'm not here for breakfast, my maid'll have to cope. It'll be a lesson for 'er. I'll just go an' tell her. Then I'll join you. And at least, even though it's the middle of the night, that star'll make it light enough for us to see our way. Best put my boots on though, for the road.'

'Thanks, Sal.'

Andrea Sarginson took up creative writing on retirement. She is inspired by her past experiences: almost twenty years in NHS nursing, fourteen of which included nursing in the Territorial Army; studying and teaching the history of art, especially Christian art; and the spirituality of Christianity. She is an Authorised Lay Minister in the Manchester Diocese.

The Midwife

Helen Murray

I HEARD that his mother held him in her arms after they killed him. It broke my heart into a thousand pieces; imagining her tears falling onto his bloody cheeks, the tenderness with which she smoothed his hair after they untangled the thorns. The way she pulled him to her breast as if she could become one with him again, the way she had once before carried him under her heart. I heard in my mind the broken sobs as she rocked back and forth in the kind of agony only a mother could feel with her child lifeless in her arms.

I'll start at the beginning.

I'm a midwife.

It was an ordinary afternoon in Bethlehem when the innkeeper's wife knocked on my door. All the women knew where to find me. She had two boys, the youngest of whom I'd helped her bring into the world a month before. She told me there was a young woman and her husband lodging with them whose time was near and no family to help. Of course, I'd come. What else would I do?

At first it seemed just like any other. I saw a young girl flushed with anticipation and apprehension, in the intermittent throes of birth pains. A man pacing; awkward and startled and useless like they all are. He was happy to make himself scarce.

She gratefully followed my advice, eyes wide as she listened, then squeezed tight shut as she gripped my hand and her body did what it was created to do. When her boy arrived the tears came, as always. She held him in her arms and smoothed his wisps of dark hair and spoke love into him as he cried a good, strong, healthy wail. I will never tire of those first moments!

With all my ladies, I make sure they're looked after and

everything is as it should be before the anxious husband returns and I take my leave. It's not a time for strangers, but as I made to go she reached for me and pulled me close and kissed my cheek. As I leaned down close to the baby boy cradled in her arms I felt an overwhelming emotion that I had never felt before. A connection.

She whispered her thanks and as her eyes found mine it was as if she was sharing a secret. I could not fathom it. I laid my trembling fingers gently on the boy's head and whispered my blessing and her smile will stay with me forever. I remember everything of that moment. The cool breeze, the shifting and blowing of the cattle, the spikiness of the straw, the flush of exertion on her neck and the way that her hair curled into ringlets with perspiration.

I saw the star later that night. People stared and marvelled. Sleep was out of the question so I sat up and wondered and asked God what it could mean. I heard later that because of that star, visitors crowded into that cramped place and knelt in front of the young mother, bewildered husband and her precious baby boy.

I brought many babies into the world after that; each one beautiful and God-sent, but none like this. I realised later that if I had never delivered another, I would have completed my life's work that night.

I realised it years later when a man called Jesus came to town and practically everyone went out onto the hillside to listen. He was something special; some said he was a teacher like no other; a long-awaited prophet, maybe. Some even said he was the Messiah. He was here, in our town, teaching. Friends came to find me. Of course I would go. What else would I do?

He wasn't like the other preachers. Nothing much to look at, you know, but his eyes were unforgettable; they could see into your soul, I swear it. Others say the same: the good, the bad, the things you'd like to hide; Jesus saw right through who you were, the darkest depths of you—and still those eyes were full of love.

I sat all day in the hot sun, despite my old body and aching joints. I was captivated. He spoke gently and fiercely. Plainly and in riddles. He challenged and confused us, but the deepest part of me responded to the truth of his words. I felt that strange, overwhelming connection once again. He spoke of God the Father and the Kingdom of Heaven as if he knew them intimately and I knew that the time had come to make a decision. I believed him. I believed *in* him.

It was then that I saw her. Her face softer, lines of age around her eyes and mouth. She sat on the edge of the crowd, watchful, with a gentle smile as he taught and blessed and held children on his knee. He moved close to her at one point and his fingers grazed her shoulder in a gesture of such tenderness I realised that she was his mother, and that I knew them both. My breath caught in my throat and I thought my heart would stop.

I was back all those years—the night of the stars. The stable with straw and the placid cattle. A sweet girl with whispered gratitude and eyes that spoke of promises and secrets.

The ordinary, extraordinary baby that I caught in my arms and wrapped in cloths and placed on her breast.

Jesus Christ.

Not much longer after that I saw her face again in my mind when I heard what happened. Those knowing, faith-filled eyes again closed tight in pain as she cradled her son to her breast for a second time. The beginning and the end.

And yet not the end. A rebirth three days later, they say, with no need for a midwife.

He lives.

Emmanuel. God with us. Always.

Helen Murray lives in Derbyshire, England and has a blog, Are We Nearly There Yet? *(www.hmarewenearlythereyet.blogspot.com) where she writes about life and faith.*

A Children's Carol

Ros Bayes

Baby Jesus lay sleeping so peaceful and warm,
And Mary, his mother shared his peace and calm.
The great God almighty, so humble and small,
He laid down his glory to come to us all.

He who put all the planets and stars in their place
Came bringing a message of God's love and grace,
The wise men and shepherds felt his touch of peace;
This child brought their spirits new joy and release.

Baby Jesus no longer lies warm in the hay;
He is no defenceless young infant today.
Yet still in our lives we are touched by his love,
And he stills our turmoil with peace like a dove.

Saviour Jesus, your birth changed our history's course,
And in human lives you give peace for remorse.
Fill me with your Spirit, make me more like you,
And help me in my life to spread your peace, too.

❈

Ros Bayes has written fifteen books including 'A' level text books, books on disability and devotional books, as well as several dozen magazine articles. She is currently working on her third novel. She is the Training Resources Developer for the Christian disability charity Through the Roof.

A Children's Carol

Ros Bayes

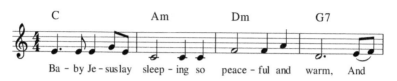

Ba - by Je - sus lay sleep - ing so peace - ful and warm, And

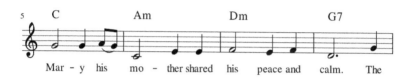

Mar - y his mo - ther shared his peace and calm. The

great God al - might - y so hum - ble and small, He

laid down his glor - y to come to us all.

The Nativity

Animals and Shepherds

Gloria & Archie's Nativity Story

Kirsty Wyllie

IT all began on a clear night in Bethlehem when Mr Thomas left his sheep to go into town. 'Where's he going?' asked Gloria the sheep, who was expecting her fifth lamb. Disappearing Shepherds weren't part of her delivery plan.

'He's going to see the new baby,' replied Archie the sheep. 'It all happened last night when he met three men in robes. I don't know what all the fuss is about.'

The look on Gloria's face was one of surprise. 'He must think it's important enough to leave us in the lurch. What did the men say? Could you hear anything?'

Archie took offence at her comment. 'Of course, I could hear. I'm not going deaf you know.'

'I didn't mean it like that!' Gloria laughed.

Archie continued, 'The tallest man asked Mr Thomas if they could sit down and rest with him for a while. He agreed and asked if they would like a refreshing glass of water. I've never seen a human gulp down water so fast.'

Gloria's fascination was evident. 'Where did the men come from?'

'The fat one told Mr Thomas that they were Magi—whatever that is.' Archie shook his woolly head. 'They'd travelled far from a place called Babylon. I remember thinking, why go to all that trouble?'

My question was soon answered when the smallest of the men said they were simply following the stars and were in search of someone called the Messiah. I don't know what they were talking about, but the shepherd sure did.

'He became all excited and began jumping up and down, followed by pacing up and down the field. I've no idea what was wrong with him. Then I fell asleep and the next thing I remember is waking up to you asking me where is he going.'

Gloria suddenly realised she knew something about where Mr Thomas had gone. 'Oh! I know where he is.'

An amazed look flashed across Archie's face. 'How come you know and I don't?'

'It all happened when you were asleep!' she laughed. 'A man draped in white and bathed in light appeared. Mr Thomas was terrified. The man told him not to fear for he was an Angel and that the son of God had been born in a humble stable. Born for everyone not just Royalty.'

Archie, without a second thought, told Gloria that they should go and see the baby boy too. Gloria was thrilled with this idea. They gathered up various offspring and set off in search of the baby. The sheep family took what seemed like days to walk along the grassy pastures. Suddenly out of nowhere they caught sight of a single bright star in the sky shining down onto the old town stable behind the Bethlehem Inn.

Archie, leading his family over the last hill before reaching the stable, heard a low groan of pain from Gloria.

'It's coming Archie! Our baby is coming!' she said, breathing heavily.

Archie stopped on the spot, turned around and calmly answered her, 'I'll go ahead with the children and let Mr Thomas know. We'll give you some space.'

'Okay. Good idea!' she said with a smile followed by a yelp of discomfort.

Archie took the children into the stable and Gloria found a dry patch of grass where she allowed nature take its course. Before too long her new lamb was born and Mr Thomas arrived to find her cleaning her baby.

He took both of them up in his arms and carried them into the warmth of the stable where with her newborn lamb, Anna, Gloria could see for herself the baby boy who had generated so much talk.

A beautiful young woman who Gloria and Archie imagined to be the child's mother was apparently called Mary. She and the man sitting beside her, Joseph, her husband, had given the baby boy the name of Jesus.

Gloria lay on the soft warm straw amongst the horses and pigs with her family whilst Mr Thomas kept hold of Anna. He had the biggest smile on his face and everyone in that stable felt special as they witnessed the miracle of that first Christmas day.

Kirsty Wyllie enjoys celebrating Christmas by capturing the true seasonal spirit with her festive work.

Commotion in the Courtyard

Nicky Copeland

THE week started pretty much like any other. The humans went about their work—the man was up early every morning and went off to work in the fields nearby. The woman washed the clothes, prepared the meals and looked after the children. They have three—two boys and a girl. They're still quite young—one of the boys hasn't yet been weaned. The older two are always running around, making lots of noise. Their mother is always trying to get them to help with the chores, but they're too small—they just want to play. It was business as usual for us animals, too. My role, as a goat, is to provide milk. It's not a bad life—I'm taken out to graze regularly, and they treat me well.

Earlier this week, things started to get quite busy in our village. I heard them talking about a census or something. Anyway, lots of people have come to stay in the house. It's packed. And we animals are playing host to some visiting donkeys too. Not that we mind—it's a nice change from the usual routine.

Last night, a young couple came to the house. They seemed quite desperate. Even I could see she was heavily pregnant, and from what I gather, they'd travelled a long way, from a place called Nazareth. It would have taken them several days to get here. That's an exhausting journey for anyone, let alone a woman who's about to have a baby.

Anyway, they were hoping to stay with the family. They're distant relatives, so it's the obvious thing to do. The only problem was that the house was already bursting at the seams. What were they going to do?

I overheard the conversation between the man of the house and the travellers. He felt awful that he had no room for them inside the house. The only thing he could offer them, he said, was to sleep in the courtyard with the animals! Now, as I said, we're happy to entertain visitors, but we've never had human visitors in our little courtyard before. We felt quite honoured. I'm not sure how they would have felt about it, though. We're not exactly the cleanest and quietest of roommates, and—not to put too fine a point on it—it's pretty smelly here, and you have to watch where you walk, if you know what I mean ...

They're an amazing couple. They didn't complain, even though the woman looked all in. They made themselves as comfortable as they could and settled down for the night. They were talking quietly before they went to sleep, and I discovered that their names were Joseph and Mary.

A little while later, I was woken up by a dreadful commotion. There were women everywhere, and I realised Mary was having her baby. My heart went out to her. She must still have been worn out from all that travelling, and now she was having to muster all her strength to give birth. I've had a few kids myself, so I know how it feels, although it always seems as though it's much harder for humans to give birth than animals. I don't know why.

A few hours later, I heard a newborn cry. I'd recognise that sound anywhere—I've been around for a few human births. A boy—how wonderful! It's such a special moment when you lay eyes on your newborn for the first time. The miracle of birth—it never gets old—whether it's your own baby or someone else's. Awesome!

The woman wrapped the baby in some strips of cloth and laid him in our feeding trough. I was about to be indignant. What a cheek! What about our breakfast?! But then I saw him. He's just an ordinary human baby, yet there's something about him—something different, something very special. I can't quite work out what it is, but there's definitely something.

The man, Joseph, was delighted. He's such a gentle man and is devoted to his wife. I heard them say something about him not being the child's natural father—I don't really understand that—but he was delighted nonetheless and promised faithfully he would look after them.

Eventually, all the excitement settled down and everyone went back to bed. Mary and Joseph stayed awake for a while. They were totally besotted with their baby. They said they were going to call him Jesus. It means 'to save'. A perfect name for a very special baby. Very fitting, if you ask me. They said something about an angel having given them the name.

We'd just settled down again when a group of visitors arrived: shepherds from the nearby fields. As if there weren't enough people here already! They said they'd come to visit the baby. How did they know about him so soon—he's only just been born—and why on earth would they want to visit him? They're not related—they don't even know the family!

Well, the story gets even stranger. It turns out these shepherds had been visited by some angels who told them the Messiah has been born. So, they left their sheep and rushed to see him for themselves. They were blown away—and so were Mary and Joseph!

If this baby really is the Messiah, then he truly is very special. The humans have been waiting for him for centuries. There have been many prophecies about him, so I can understand their excitement! What I don't understand, though, is that if he really is their Messiah, why on earth was he born in a courtyard, with us animals for company? Why wasn't he born in a palace? Why such lowly beginnings for such an important person?

So many questions, and I'll probably never know the answers. One thing I do know, though: this baby is going to change the world.

❋

Among the many hats that Nicki Copeland wears are those of wife, mum, nanny, speaker, writer, editor and eater of chocolate. She loves to encourage others to throw off everything that holds them back and embrace the freedom God is offering. She is the author of Losing the Fig Leaf *and* Less Than Ordinary?

The Donkey's Tale

Nikki Salt

THE soft breeze tickles my ears as I stare at millions of bright shining stars. My mother told me about the Great Maker. How he sculpted every single star, just as he designed and formed every living creature. All with love. They wink at me, as though wishing me well for tomorrow. *Tomorrow*. A small frisson of fear runs down my back. The day I leave my mother to work for a new master. I nudge her for comfort and she responds with a gentle bray.

'Don't worry, little one. The Great Maker will protect you. I'm sure your new master will treat you kindly.'

I flick my tail at an inquisitive fly. 'Tell me about the birth of the King, Mama.'

'Again, sweet one?'

'I like to hear you tell it, Mama,' I plead.

She rubs her velvet nose against my head and I imagine the smile in her eyes.

'I was about your age,' she began. 'Young and strong, when my then master started preparing for a long journey. How bad-tempered and irritable I became as I watched him collect belongings. Heavy, lumpy, awkward possessions that I would have to carry. I stamped my hoof, tossed my head and swished my tail. I didn't want to leave the lush northern highlands of Galilee where the grass was sweet. But my master, a patient man, cajoled me into carrying everything. That early September morning, petulant and cranky, I left my lush paddock, laden up like a common beast of burden,' she broke off and laughed. 'I had a rather high opinion of myself in those days. Mary, my master's charming wife, walked by my side, chatting merrily, pointing out flowers and plants and feeding me donkey delicacies along the way. Whenever we came upon water, she would insist on stopping so I could drink. In spite of the heavy packs, I began to enjoy myself, but as the days progressed I noticed Mary became quieter. I nuzzled her hand, hoping for a piece of pomegranate, but she clutched my mane to steady herself, her other hand lying protectively across her abdomen. I had seen jennies heavy with foal, and I realised Mary was carrying her own foal.'

'A foal, mama?' I snort laughter through my nose.

'A human foal.' She stroked my cheek with her cool nose. 'A baby. Mary stumbled along the track, barely able to put one foot in front of the other. Anger surged through me. I picked up my pace and head-butted my master's rear end. That woke him up! He had a few choice words for me, but at least he noticed poor Mary and helped her onto my back.'

'Was she heavy, Mama?' I ask the question, though I know her answer.

'That's the strange thing, my son. The child within looked ready to birth, yet I barely noticed her weight.

'After many days of travel, we arrived in Bethlehem and my master began searching for lodgings. I'd never seen so many humans. Some were trying to sell us things, others jostled to get past us, and oh, the noise. Finally, I lifted my head and brayed my loudest, if only to hear my own voice. Mary shushed me and led me to a water trough while the master appeared to be arguing with an innkeeper. As I drank, Mary gasped and grabbed my neck as though in great pain. Well, I'd had enough. That poor girl needed to rest. I planted my four hooves firmly into the dusty ground, while she buried her head in my neck, panting. The master's shoulders sagged as he joined us but put his arm around his wife. His said not to worry, they'd find shelter, but I saw that his face did not believe his words. He tugged at my rope and thumped my rump, but I stood firm. I would not put Mary through another minute of travel. Couldn't the master see her exhaustion? We would rest here. I turned to make myself a little more comfortable and bumped against a wooden door. It swung open and I brayed in delight at what I can only describe as a palace fit for a king. Far superior to my own snug shelter back in Galilee, fresh straw littered the floor and a manger overflowed with hay and kitchen scraps. Without hesitation, I pushed towards the food trough and sank my nose into the heavenly, aromatic feast. Mary, following me, sank into the hay with a small cry.

'That night, Mary had her baby.'

I prick my ears longing to hear the last few words of the story yet not wanting it to end. 'Yes, Mama,' I whisper into the night.

'I know I watched the King being born. The King of all the universe.'

'How do you know, Mama?' I ask with a shiver.

'When I laid eyes on that baby, I knew. And ...'

'Yes, Mama?'

'I long to see him again. The King of the universe, Son of the Great Maker.' She nuzzles me. 'Now, go to sleep, sweet one. Tomorrow is a big day.'

I dig my hooves into the sand, refusing to move. 'I'm not leaving you, Mama,' I bray. 'I want to hear your stories about the King of the universe.'

The two men, attempting to lead me from the paddock, throw their hands up in defeat and put a rope around my mother's neck.

'The new masters are taking us both, son.'

Somewhat mollified, I allow the men to guide us out of the village towards the main road to Jerusalem. 'Where are we going?'

My mother ignores my question. 'It's Him,' she whispers.

'Who?' I see the crowds shouting something about Hosanna. I feel people drape their cloaks over my back. A man approaches and suddenly I know too. 'It's You,' I bray as He climbs onto my back. I'm carrying the King of the universe, Son of the Great Maker.

❖

Nikki Salt lives in a rickety old house, in the middle of a field full of cabbages with her husband, two kids and various other animals. Passionate about children's writing, she's currently filling her debut novel for kids with colourful characters and extraordinary adventures.

The True Meaning of Christmas

Sophie Neville

And the angel said to them, 'Fear not, for behold, I bring you good news of great joy that will be for all the people. For unto you is born this day in the city of David a Savior, who is Christ the Lord. And this will be a sign for you: you will find a baby wrapped in swaddling cloths and lying in a manger.'

Luke 2:10–12

I'M sure you know what to do with a tea towel. If you tie it around someone's head, you can turn them into a shepherd. This works well at Christmas if you live in a culture that appreciates nativity plays. It enables you to ask: Why did the angel of the Lord bring news of the Messiah's birth to those engaged in caring for very stupid animals? Was everyone else drinking at the inn?

In those days, shepherds were regarded as the lowest of the low. They would normally be uneducated, hired hands, banned from synagogues and obliged, by law, to graze sheep in the wilderness. The Jewish authorities labelled sheep-herders 'ritually unclean' since they could not avoid treading in dung or handling dead animals. However, theirs was a responsible job. They were trusted with the wealth of others, the equivalent of people's savings plans, pensions and bank accounts, which could be moved around and traded easily. Milked daily and sold for their meat, wool and skins, sheep constituted a productive investment that increased as they bred. As each lambing season came around, the shepherds, who encountered the joy of new life, would value and protect the precious young—unlike King Herod.

In England we drive sheep with dogs, but Palestinian shepherds led their sheep from one pasture to another and went out with rod and staff to look for any lost. They needed to be tough. Persistence was required to keep the flock together and guide them to water. The fat-tailed sheep reared in Israel would give birth from November onwards when herds were vulnerable to being scattered by predators. Keeping donkeys or dogs helped keep foxes away, but not thieves.

Abraham, Jacob and Moses were all shepherds. David, the shepherd boy from Bethlehem, became Israel's greatest king. Ezekiel prophesied that Jesus would be the Good Shepherd who would search for strays, rescue and gather the lost; the one to strengthen the weak, heal the sick and bind up the injured. While we shove with flank and shoulder, he promises showers of blessing and a covenant of peace.

Scholars say the shepherds living in the fields below Bethlehem were different from others. They were employed by the High Priest. Some think they could have been Levites ordained to select animals for sacrificial purposes. They probably congregated at Midal Edar, a thousand paces from Bethlehem. This 'Tower of the Flock' mentioned in the Book of Micah, is where Rachel gave birth to Benjamin. Here, a newborn lamb chosen for sacrifice would be wrapped in strips of cloth known as swaddling bands and lain in a depression in the limestone rock known as 'the manger' to keep it clean and prevent it from getting blemished.

Every day, two male lambs were sacrificed as the 'Tameed' or 'continual burnt offering' at the temple. In the thirty days before Passover, huge numbers of year-old male lambs belonging to the High Priest were gathered outside Bethlehem before being taken to Jerusalem, six miles north, to be sacrificed or eaten in commemoration of the Passover when Jews and Samaritans remember how God delivered them from slavery in Egypt.

There would have been quite a number of trustworthy shepherds living in the fields, to look after them around the clock. It was to these working men that God chose to declare news of the Messiah's arrival on Earth. What would they have thought of the great company of the heavenly host who appeared with the angel? How would they have described it to the High Priest who employed them?

The glimpse of heaven recorded in Luke's Gospel is treasured by men on whom God's favour rests and yet we only read this account once a year, usually when we are stressed out by the pressure of choosing presents or decorating fir trees. Perhaps we should take time to contemplate the night sky instead of rushing about shopping. Angels must be terrifying. They left Daniel and Zachariah gripped with fear. Mary, who had met the angel Gabriel in Nazareth nine months earlier, must have been reassured by the shepherds' story, especially after giving birth in what was probably a filthy stable. Some say Jesus may have been born at Midal Edar and laid in the limestone manger. The shepherds would have known this spot and hurried there without hesitation. Whatever the exact location, it was likely to have been ritually unclean.

One of the best things about Christmas is that it has become a family occasion. Expectations rise, friends gather and show their love for each other, making an effort to reach out to the lonely. We serve God by ministering to our children and making proper use of tea towels. What more can we do? Perhaps remember the Lord Jesus put an end to the need for animal sacrifice as we try not to incinerate our turkey? Should we sing in the open air like angels, ringing out heavenly bells? What would it mean to leave our flock and hurry off to spread the word concerning what we have been told? The shepherds did. Have a chat to those still crowded into the inn. They might come to midnight Mass. Christmas is an undeniable public relations opportunity for Christians.

The meaning of Christ's birth would have been instantly

recognised by shepherds as soon as they saw the baby Jesus. They got the message. It was the pure, spotless lamb, wrapped in swaddling bands and laid in a manger, that was chosen as a sacrifice for the forgiveness of sins.

Sophie Neville is a speaker for the Bible Society and President of The Arthur Ransome Society, often giving talks on her career in film and television. She published a series of memoirs entitled The Making of Swallows and Amazons *(1974),* Funnily Enough *and* Ride the Wings of Morning *before winning the Athanatos novel-writing prize in 2017 for* Makorongo's War. *www.sophieneville.net*

An Old Shepherd Remembers

Pauline West

How come we never saw the thorns;
the spikes;
the threats;
the inbuilt desperation?

There was too much to wonder at.
The angels,
the light,
the young girl and her child.

How could we know?

We thought our life was hard,
but we heard he had it harder.
Crucified said some.
It was the way they ruled;
it happened.

But not to his sort!
One born with so much promise;
so much presence;
it took our breath away.

If I thought he'd hear
I'd ask God—why?
Was he really meant for stable?
or for cross?

I'm old now,
too old for watching sheep.
I clean the stable,
fetch the straw,
fill the manger –

and when I'm done …
I swear I see him there again;
hear his thanks;
see his nail-pierced hands stretched out to me.

And I remember
and kneel once more to worship him.

Pauline West is a retired Baptist minister and member of the Baptist Union Retreat Group currently living in the Lake District. She creates visual displays for reflection based in two local chapels and writes pieces that express her faith experience in daily living and observation.

The Nativity

In the Inn

The Last Room

Andrew Tawn

THE census was a nuisance. The last thing I needed was a journey to Bethlehem. My days were full of business and profit; there was no room in my life for a trip to that God-forsaken place.

I set off late from Jerusalem, waiting to tie up a deal. It was winter and with the early darkness came a biting wind, so I was glad to reach the lamps and the shelter of the streets of Bethlehem, mean as they were. However, the place was full of visitors and I swear the room I found was the very last room in the very last inn in town. I suppose I should have been grateful, but I was full of my own importance. This was not the kind of accommodation I was used to, and I made sure the innkeeper knew it.

I had just agreed to take the room when there was a knocking behind me on the door to the inn. As the innkeeper opened the door, I glimpsed a young couple dressed in the lowly clothes of country dwellers.

'I'm sorry,' I heard the innkeeper say. 'I have no rooms left. Unless …Just wait a minute.'

He closed the door and turned to me.

'There is a stable,' he said, and paused. 'Perhaps … you might …?'

'That is fortunate for them,' I replied, pretending not to understand his meaning. 'It is a cold night for them to spend on the streets.'

'But she is expecting a child,' he said, 'and her time is near.'

'What has that to do with me?' I asked, full of indignation.

I did not sleep that night. The inn was noisy. The bed was uncomfortable. I lay there, outraged at the innkeeper's insolence.

In Jerusalem where I was known for my wealth and success, no one would have dared suggest such a thing to me, Joseph of Arimathea.

The night wore on. Gradually all became quiet. Still I tossed and turned. I was there first. There were other guests. Why should they not give up their rooms? Why me?

I discovered the next morning that the girl had given birth. I thought of her suffering the pains of labour in the chill of the stable. I wondered what sort of life could lie in prospect for a child born amongst the dung and smell and breath of animals. I began to regret keeping the last room for myself. For the first time, I recognised my selfishness and I was ashamed.

I left early to avoid the couple. I could not face them. In denying them a room for the birth of their child I felt I had denied love and life itself. On the road back to Jerusalem, I looked at my life, so full of business and profit and my own importance. And I saw how empty it was.

Over the years since then I have made room in my heart for the poor and the lowly, and my soul has been filled with peace. Except for one thing. If only I could have met that child who was born in the stable, and made some amends for my selfishness that night. I feared the sting of guilt would go with me to my grave.

But now, thirty years on, I have the chance I prayed for. A man was crucified in Jerusalem today. The city has been full of rumours about him. Some said he was a prophet. Some even claimed he was the Messiah. I might have paid little attention but for one story: they say he was born in Bethlehem, in a stable, because there was no room at the inn.

I could not save him from death. My influence with the Roman governor is not so great as that. But I did ask Pilate for his body. Outside the city I owned a tomb, newly carved out of rock in readiness for my burial. I laid the body of Jesus there.

It seemed but a poor reparation, that I who denied him a room at his birth should provide a last room at his death. But now I find that death has lost its sting. For my tomb is full of the one who is love; and there is room in my heart for God.

After 23 years as a parish priest, Andrew Tawn now organises clergy training for the Anglican diocese of Leeds. He likes to use stories to communicate the gospel, though finds them much harder to write than sermons. He is author of a book of acrostic name prayers, Naming and Blessing *(2010).*

Shining Like Stars

Annmarie Miles

AS I lay down in comfort, I felt a pang of guilt thinking of the heavily pregnant girl and her exhausted husband sleeping on the floor of my cattle shed. Later, my wife Hannah and I woke to the cries of the girl; without a word, Hannah got up and dressed. Before she left the room, she held out her hand to me. I pulled her close and placed my hand on her swollen belly. 'Will you scream like that when your time comes?'

'Louder,' she smiled, kissing my hand before leaving.

I lay still, listening to the intermittent cries of the girl until a smile overtook my face at the sound of the baby's cry. I wondered how I could feel such warmth and joy at the birth of a stranger. Soon after, Hannah returned. 'It's a boy, Malachi,' she laughed, and we hugged as if it was our own.

I looked at Hannah as she lay down to sleep; she had never looked so beautiful. She was radiant.

We were woken again by voices outside our window. We had slept sounder and longer than usual and rushed to tend to our guests, but everyone was outside. Some were hovering around the stable door, some were in groups whispering, others were laughing and shouting.

'Shepherds? Just shepherds.'

'I don't know, they've gone now, but they were telling the truth. You could see it in their eyes.'

'Angels? Did they actually see angels?'

'Yes, they saw them. And they sang, the most beautiful singing.'

'About the baby in Malachi's stable? Surely not.'

'Joseph and Mary are their names.'

'They knelt down before the baby, like he was King David himself.'

For the next few days, there was much activity in and around the stable, but things quietened down. Unlike most of the visitors who stayed only as long as required for the census, the little family didn't go home, ending up in lodgings not far from us. They became a familiar part of the community, and after a while most of us forgot the shepherds' wondrous declarations. Hannah spent a lot of time with the baby and his mother, especially after our own child was born. A girl, whom Hannah begged me to call 'Mary.' How could I say no to her? She was alive with light after every visit with her new friend.

Life was just settling down to the new normality when more changes were heralded by another sleepless night. This time because of a bright star moving ever closer to the village, eventually resting almost over our home. It shone day and night, like a sun that refused to set. More chatter in the marketplace spoke of travellers who looked like foreign Royalty, making their way towards us. That evening we all stood in silence as the rich strangers entered the village. Some of us recalled the visit of the shepherds and their celebrations. How could we have forgotten that night so easily. The visitors stood before our friend Mary, who was holding her son, and bowed low, then presented her with extravagant gifts. They stayed a short while, then they were gone. Hannah wanted to go to Mary and Joseph to find out about the strangers and the gifts they had given, but I urged her to leave them alone until the following day.

The next morning Hannah and our little Mary were out of bed by the time I woke up. I found them in Mary and Joseph's home. Hannah was sitting on the floor, crying.

'They're gone,' Hannah wept.

It was true. No one knew why, or where, but Joseph, Mary and their child had disappeared in the night. The information-mongers in the market spread word Herod himself was looking for them.

I have no words to describe the days that followed. Herod's men brought down on us such aggression and devastation I cannot speak of and will never forget. Our daughter was spared, but we were surrounded by grief on every side, and it quenched the light in Hannah. She grieved the disappearance of her friend and the bereavement of many neighbours. Maybe it was Hannah's sadness or my inability to change it, but eventually our daughter Mary left us too. She had grown into a feisty teenager who would not be tamed. One day we woke up and she was gone.

More years of sadness followed, and I gave up hope of ever seeing my wife shine again. I heard rumours of the Messiah in Jerusalem and without telling Hannah why, I made arrangements to be there in time for the Passover. But by the time we were there and settled, it was all over. The man they were calling the Messiah had been arrested, tried and executed. I was frustrated. Instead of coming to a place of light, a place where Hannah might find some peace, it was a place of darkness and loss.

I did not go to the centre of the city until the Feast of Pentecost. It was pandemonium, but it was beautiful. The excitement, the truth, the hope. I wanted Hannah to know it too, it was what she needed. I turned to run back to get her— and there they were. In the middle of the crowd stood our two Marys. Unmistakable; their faces shining brighter than the star all those years ago. With tears and laughter, we ran to Hannah. Their excited greetings and embraces brought more laughter and tears. Hannah was instantly transformed, as was I. Not just by the reunion. The star of Bethlehem shone again, this time in our hearts, as we listened to the story of the baby born in our stable, who became the risen Messiah. Our broken years were restored to us, our friend returned to us and our lost daughter found. Who could have foretold how that night in Bethlehem would change our lives, and light up our world, forever.

Annmarie Miles is from Dublin, Ireland. She lives with her husband Richard who is a pastor in the Eastern Valley of Gwent, in South Wales. She writes short stories, magazine articles, devotional pieces for Christian radio, and blogs about her faith at www.auntyamo.com

No Room at the Inn
A dramatic sketch

Brian Vincent

PROPS:
Chair and telephone

(Man picks up phone and dials.)

MAN:

Hello? Is that reception? Good. This is the Penthouse suite. I'd like to order dinner for 8 o'clock. I'll have the pâté as a starter, followed by the braised steak Siciliana with a selection of vegetables. Then, for sweet, I think meringues chantilly and coffee. Oh, I nearly forgot, also a bottle of your best Italian wine. And would you tell room service to make sure the wine is chilled?

(Pause)

Thank you, yes, the suite is very comfortable and the view over Bethlehem is magnificent. This must be one of your best rooms. It's just what I wanted.

(Pause)

Sorry, what did you say? Would I be prepared to share the suite with another family? Are you serious? Frankly I'm afraid I wouldn't. It's been tiresome enough to interrupt my hectic business schedule to journey here to register for the census, without having to slum it with a family of peasants. I've been travelling for days and I need to relax …

I think you're forgetting I was careful to make arrangements in advance. I booked and paid—handsomely I might add—for a lounge, dressing room, bedroom with en suite bathroom, and satellite TV. That's what I asked for and that is what I've got, and

I see no reason to share it with the feckless masses. Like me they should have come prepared. There was plenty of warning.

(Pause)

I appreciate the town is crowded with people flocking in from everywhere ... I don't like your implication that it would be the charitable thing to do. I think I do more than my fair share for charity. I regularly buy a weekly lottery ticket and I always drop a coin into a beggar's bowl as I pass. I pray for the poor when I go to worship and I give generously into the collection plate. In addition, I pay my taxes, so please don't lecture me on what I should do for charity. I think I've earned my place in heaven. God helps those who help themselves, that's what I say. Charity begins at home.

(Pause)

Did you say the woman's pregnant? Well now! Isn't that just typical? These people breed like rabbits and then they expect everybody else to bail them out. It wouldn't surprise me to learn that she's not married and no doubt the man she's with is not the baby's father.

(Pause)

I thought as much. Haven't these people heard of family planning? Isn't there somewhere else you can put them?

(Pause)

Every room's full? Well, what about one of the sheds at the back of the hotel? I'm sure they'd feel at home in one of them.

(Pause)

Look! I'm not interested in how they are, who they are, or where they've come from. I'm only interested in a little peace and quiet, a pleasant meal and a good night's sleep, so please don't bother me anymore. And don't forget I'm expecting dinner at 8 o'clock.

(Slams down phone)

Whatever next? Just who do these people think they are?

NARRATOR (Voice-over)

Approximately seven hundred years before the birth of Jesus,

Isaiah, the Hebrew prophet proclaimed these words: 'For to us a child is born, to us a son is given; and the government shall be upon his shoulder, and his name shall be called Wonderful Counselor, Mighty God, Everlasting Father, Prince of Peace. Of the increase of his government and peace there will be no end, on the throne of David and over his kingdom, to establish and to uphold it with justice and with righteousness from this time forth and forevermore.' (Isaiah 9:6–7)

Brian Vincent has been a Christian for forty years and enjoys using his writing to excite people about the good news of Jesus. He has had many short stories and articles published in the secular marketplace and hopes their content reflects Christian values.

The Innkeeper

Fran Hill

HIS eyes have met mine many times in the last hour and it's true what people say about his gaze. You feel searched, found wanting, yet still loved. He knows me, I think, even though we have never met. Can I put my hope in him? I wonder, and then my body slumps with the disappointment of it, the weight of it.

I've left it too late, surely.

Bethlehem had fizzed that night. People herded into the town for the census, seeking out inns like mine, or spare rooms and corners of rooms.

My young wife had tugged my sleeve as I'd carried lamb with spices to guests. 'Bartholomew,' she'd said, her voice hoarse with hope. 'We will be *rich* by the morning. I can buy that purple cloak from the market. Some sandals to match?'

'My love,' I said. 'Slow down—'

'But, Bartholomew,' she said, her deep brown eyes wide with persuasion. 'Add to tonight's takings the money from the group of men who take our back room each week for their meetings ...'

'Ssh, wife.' I put a finger on her lips. 'Be wise, and quiet. I'm not sure what that group discusses. And I don't want to know. How did I let you persuade me to take that booking?'

'But with their money, and tonight's bounty!' She giggled, reminding me of when I'd first met her, a girl of fifteen, raw and beautiful, but already in love with the bright and the new. A bracelet here. A hair decoration there.

She was right, though. I'd needed another money bag in

which to stuff the coins as people shouldered their way in, dragging bags, children, spare blankets for comfort. Each time I served someone with a drink, there was another knock, and as I answered the door, a call from inside the house, 'Innkeeper! More meat, please.' Or 'This room is not clean!' Our own small children were given simple duties, and I'd sent for Thomas the olive grower's son to help serve. The inn was filled with talk, babies crying, men in a corner playing a game with counters and surprise moves.

'It feels a significant night,' I'd said to my wife. 'I sense it in my bones, something stirring.'

She laughed. 'You and your stirring bones. It's the promise of money.'

'No,' I said.

At midnight, another knock came. 'I'll get it,' I said to her, 'but be it King Herod himself, there is no room.'

At the door was a man leading a donkey which carried a woman, clearly with child, and with her hands resting on her belly. Her face creased with anxiety, or perhaps pain. My own wife had nearly died in childbirth. I recalled her suffering.

'I'm sorry. I wish I could help,' I said.

The man said, 'Please. Please.'

As he said this, a deep groan came from the woman. She put her hands on her thighs and bowed her head, closing her eyes as though to shut us out and take refuge in another world of her own.

I looked behind me in case my wife heard. 'We only have the barn,' I said, 'where the animals are kept. But there's straw. I won't charge you.'

'Anything,' the man said, as the woman groaned a second time, deep and guttural.

'Don't tell my wife you're not paying,' I said. And I directed them round the back of the inn.

❦

Some months later, the back room men failed to arrive. I never saw them again.

'But they haven't paid this week's money,' my wife said.

'I don't care,' I said. 'It's dirty money, I'm sure of it. I'm pleased they've gone.'

But I was a frailer man, thirty years later, in body and in resolve. And poorer. When a band of young men thumped on the door, insisting that, as I had hosted their fathers years before, I could also host them, I gave in.

Yet again, I let men into the back room, gathered their coins, and shut my ears to their mutterings and heads-together discussions.

'Stop worrying,' my wife said. 'This way, we can eat. I can hold up my head in front of our neighbours.'

But one night, I was serving our only guest with wine when Roman soldiers thrust their way into the inn, accusing me of harbouring a group of dissidents and traitors. 'Week by week, they are here, plotting against the Roman government,' they yelled, dragging me through my own inn yard in front of my screaming wife. 'There is only one punishment for such things.'

Protesting my innocence from the back of the cart as it rumbled over uneven roads to Jerusalem only brought more whippings.

And—was I innocent?

I lost count of days. My life became rats scurrying across blackened dungeon stones, the shrieks and moans of fellow prisoners, including those I had hosted, and daily beatings. Bread as hard as walls was my only sustenance. Memories of my wife's eyes and the jangling of her bracelets kept me from praying to die.

Then, this morning, they came for me. I thought it was freedom. I stumbled behind them on weakened legs, blinking at the sudden sun.

❄

That gaze again. His eyes are dull now, but they speak as lips do. I'm on his right. The rebel to the left of him hurls insults. 'Aren't you the Messiah? Save yourself and us!'

I see his thorn-crowned head droop. With the onset of death, or with sorrow at the man's words? Either way, I know I have only seconds.

'Jesus,' I say. My voice is barely there. 'Remember me.' I'm convinced he won't hear.

'Today,' he says, his eyes fading to dark hollows, 'you will be with me in Paradise.'

I know it to be true. I don't know how I know, but I do.

He will make room for me.

❄

Fran Hill is a writer and English teacher from Warwickshire. She writes fiction, non-fiction and poetry, and her first book Being Miss *is available on Kindle and in paperback. Her website will tell you more: www.franhill. co.uk*

Daughter of the Innkeeper

Kathryn Price

OH, it was busy. Father wasn't rubbing his hands with glee any more, as he had done when the census was announced; he was using them to tear his hair out. We were so full we didn't have time to think. We'd given up our own rooms and were sleeping in a corner of the courtyard. At least I was tired enough to fall asleep as soon as I lay down, never mind how unhappy I was or how scratchy the straw.

And we got fuller! Even travellers were prepared to pay for a pile of straw in the other corners. There was nowhere to stay. Then this couple arrived, weary like all the others, dusty from the road—the difference was that she was pregnant and, by the look of it, near her time.

Cousin Joseph! We hadn't seen him for years; that part of the family had last visited when Grandfather was still alive. Father was torn. He wanted to welcome a kinsman; he had to. But if Joseph's wife gave birth, that would make the place unclean for thirty days. He'd lose all the guests, and all the money he's just been raking in.

I thought Joseph's wife looked kind. Anxious, but not as worried as she could have been. I took her a drink and offered to let her sleep on my pile of straw, but Father was cross. Joseph was cross too; he'd expected a welcome in his family town. We had no space anywhere; there just wasn't any room in the inn where Joseph and Mary could be private, and they couldn't share the open space with others. It was my little brother who came up with the idea of letting them use the stable. He'd been minding travellers' donkeys. We even had a horse in with our goats, though my brother was barely tall enough to reach the reins and had been swung off his feet more than once. People laughed at him. Not me. I never laugh at my little brother. Or smile.

There was a bit of discussion about whether the animals become unclean if they were in the same place when a woman gave birth. Honestly, these stupid rules. Father was still shaking his head when I asked, 'What would Mother have done?' He was upset at that, and I knew I wasn't being fair, but Mary was my cousin now and I wanted her to be all right. Father said Joseph could take Mary into the stable and when I said I would help them, Father didn't say anything else to me. His eyes seemed bright, but he just turned his face away.

It was private. The animals didn't mind. I put their hay on the floor to have the manger ready for the baby. Joseph was having a drink with Father. I did the best I could, though I was scared my best wouldn't be good enough. I was crying, and Mary, even in her pains, asked why. She told me she would be safe and well. She spoke of an angel and a song. The baby was a boy, just like Mary said it would be. She was right about that. Was she right about everything else she said?

I'd helped with a newborn before and I know they're too little to smile. It was ages before my brother smiled. Mary said there was something different about this baby. And she didn't die as Mother did. When I laid him in the manger, I almost thought he did smile at me. And somehow, I didn't feel as sad any more.

Kathryn Price is a wife and mum with all sorts of hobbies, but mainly dog-walking whilst thinking about not having written much recently. A Methodist Local Preacher, most of her writing has to be sermons, but there are at least two unfinished novels lurking, and daft rhymes and silly sketches occasionally appear too.

The Nativity

Following the Star

Light of the World

Jane Hendra

'the morning stars sang together
and all the angels shouted for joy'

I remember
Hearing your voice at my birth
I exploded into life
As your words ignited me
A fierce and beautiful gas giant

I watched you make others
Innumerable lanterns burning across the universe
Each in our place
Meticulous design
Elegant mathematics

All the time the angels sang
Their voices spiralling in an eternal anthem
Across the solar systems
And you laughed and laughed
Enjoying their joy

Now aeons later
I continue on the course you have designed for me
But for the first time
I am closer to that tiny planet
Of which the angels speak

Though so far away
On this night my cool light

Reaches across the heavens
Silver fingers delicately awakening
Men who observe the sky

They gaze at me for hours
They pore over their charts
Night after night
Discussing and debating
Obsessed with starlight

What are they looking for?
It is of no consequence to me
They set out on an uncertain journey
Anxious and hopeful
While I continue serenely on my certain path

Each night they progress slowly
Stumbling and hesitant
Searching for a clear way
Trying to make sense of their dark world
They risk their lives to pursue my light

I lose them for a while
In some place of uncomfortable darkness
When they finally emerge and turn their faces heavenwards
I hear them shout for joy
Restored by sweet starlight

I watch them crowd into a small house
No one wants to be left outside
For a fleeting second I am jealous
Could there be anything in this dingy place
More beautiful than me?
I can't resist just one quick glance
Starlight creeping in through an open skylight

Descending over the crowd
At the centre of the room a mother and father
Bend tenderly over a baby

The baby smiles as starlight caresses his cheek
Feather-light millennia-old
His joy jogs my memory
I look again
It is you.

Of all the wonders I have seen in the universe
Nothing compares to this
How could you dear Creator
Compress your glory into a tiny babe
On this dark planet

And why would you
Lord of all
Entrust yourself to men?
Who knows what they will do
Or where this story will end?

In the radiance of the joy of this crowd
I realise my course has been perfectly planned
From the beginning to this moment
To illuminate your birth
O Light of the World.

Jane Hendra enjoys writing short stories and Christian drama; she contributes to a monthly church blog and teaches creative writing. She is the wife of one husband, the mother of three sons, the grandmother of five grandchildren, and has been a friend of Jesus for fifty years.

A Star's View of Christmas

an imaginary reflection by the Star of Bethlehem

Tracy Williamson

I'VE been guiding them for years now, the radiance of my glory lighting their paths along countless miles and across many borders. Wise men of warring nations, they've travelled together with harmonious urgency since I whispered an unfathomable dream to follow the star to seek the newborn King of the Jews.

It was I who kindled the fire within them, to find something greater, the treasure beyond all treasures, the hope that will be fulfilled. Barely understanding, they listened. My message transformed them.

Giving up everything they knew, they followed me, knowing not where I would lead them or how long the journey would take. They put themselves in my hands, these men of great human wisdom. Some even call them kings and indeed they are, so lofty is their desire to understand this universe. It was that hint of inner yearning that I sought from them. I whispered, 'Follow the star and I will lead you to the holy one, the king of kings yet born to a virgin. Bring your gifts of gold, frankincense and myrrh.'

How I love them and long for them to see the wonderful truth unfolding before their eyes. Yet, despite years of study they understand so little. They think their own knowledge shows them the meaning of the star. They don't understand that only through God can they hear God. No study or human power can ever open the door into the heavenly realm. Yet it is into that very realm that they and all mankind are to be welcomed back. O the glory of the plans of God who never stops loving His children even when they reject Him.

They are exhilarated by my glory which ever draws them

forward, but still believe that I am just a star. I so long for that day when they embrace the truth and kneel in worship and wonder.

What a desperately long journey it has been, through vast stretches of desert, stumbling over the barren rocks and dry, sinking sand. Hungry, thirsty and constantly facing death. Daily I cover them with the glory of my protection and they keep their eyes on me as I burn with my beautiful guiding light. Yet I am so much more than what they see, for is not Bright Morning Star my true name?

Do they ever consider that if a star were to step out of its place in the cosmos and travel before them in this way, the whole balance of the universe would be destroyed? Right from the beginning we set everything in its place and the tiniest atom affects the tallest mountain; the ant changes the life of the elephant. They need to look deeper, to behold the wondrous mystery that God has hidden His glory in the form of this star. Just as surely He has hidden His very life in that of a human child. They see glimpses of the truth as my light shatters the darkness before them. But they have no idea yet that I am the living manifestation of His glory. I with Him, am the Light of the world, the whisper of the Eternal.

How awesome was that moment when He, clothed in glory, filling the heavens like an inexhaustible fire, allowed Himself to become a helpless baby within a virgin's womb. I did not leave Him then, how could I, for we were part of one another? But I too had to change, so I hid myself inside the folds of His mother's care, the touch of her hand and the divine love that would soon be poured out on all mankind.

Once they feared I had gone, when the radiant light they had followed for so long disappeared and the sky became dark. How afraid they were but never can I leave them for they are the chosen forerunners of the coming glory when every knee will bow before Him.

So, I did not depart as they feared, but I had to leave just awhile for that awesome reunion; melted into the tiniest space for the most incredible of miracles. O holy moment. The Lord of Eternity birthed to a virgin, in a stable with the animals watching by. I unleashed myself then and played in the heavens with the angels, revelling in the shepherds' awe and wonder, the fire of my glory flowing from within the stable, flames of joy touching the earth as Heaven worshipped.

And now today my mission is fulfilled as at last they enter the house where He is, the Holy. They are here, and I descend and cover them with my living shekinah glory, for I am no longer hidden inside a star but am now a fire given to the heart of every man, woman and child who believes. From the eyes of the Christ Child Jesus Immanuel, I gaze and sing, as overwhelmed with my gift of holy love-joy they bow in worship.

Tracy Williamson is an author and speaker working with the Christian Ministry MBM Trust. www.mbm-ministires.org Tracy has written several books on hearing God's voice and inner transformation. Her latest book The Father's Kiss *has just been published by Authentic Media.*

The Frankincense

Lucy Marfleet

Burning hot, that day was. I
bled from the tree, my mother
flung her hands to heaven in ugly grief.
I trickled one white
tear, clinging sticky, setting
like a knuckle bone.
Until hands came
with blades and scraped and took me.
Washed me, hustled me,
sold me in a rose-stone market among gardens of men.
Peace to you.
Then I journeyed again.
It was cooler by night. I
ached in my tomb, the camels
stepping through fields and streets.
A loud palace was there
but no King.
There was whispering too (and
secret shouting).
Peace to you.
Another outing
and a small place; a
humble space. I
laughed as the tiny fingers took me,
giggled in his mouth until
his mother found me
dried me, smelt me.
I am honey and wood, lemon and pine.
Peace to you.

I am no longer mine.
A feast and singing followed,
joy filled me,
and though their words were
not the same,
they used their hands to speak.
One night the boy, his family and I
took flight in haste.
Though I was small, they
sold me.
Peace to you.
Burning hot, that day was. I
was burning too.
My perfume filling the temple,
praising God in heaven;
my smoke rising in the temple courts,
my hands lifted at last.
Peace, peace to you.

Lucy Marfleet is a writer and blogger with a passion for communicating the Bible in original ways. See more of her work at www.lucymarfleet.com.

Mine is the Kingdom

Alison Stedman

Unearthly light blazed that memorable night,
through palace windows.
Were the stars rebelling,
trying to dethrone the sun?
Travellers' shadows
flickered across my courtyard walls;
guards swung open heavy gates
releasing them back into the night.
Disturbed, fearful,
pacing with clenched fists
I watched them journey on,
deep unease taking root.

Camels strode purposefully,
confident hooves grew distant;
riders, rich silks and turbans shimmering
eastern splendour;
Hint of Sandalwood scent hung,
an unseen reminder in the air.
Saddlebags now laden with generous provisions,
hoping to ingratiate my unexpected callers.

They'd come naturally to me,
delivering alarming enquiries,
shaking my pride.
Foreigners with celestial charts and hushed tones,
an unnerving quiet confidence,
gazing up at heavenly patterns;
led by a pinpoint of light, so dazzling

that surely heaven had split open
to pierce the earth.

Despite polite bows and presents of costly spices,
their quest sent a shiver through me;
'Where is he,
born King of the Jews?'

King of the Jews,
my title!
Not born, but given by Rome;
false smile froze,
masking jealousy beneath.

'No, a baby, destined from birth,
he is the one we must worship.'
This unknown child full of treason,
threatening to steal my reign,
stirred up anger from deep within.

'Come in, let us talk some more.'
Servants summoned, brought wine,
food to lavish upon them,
even dragged in the snivelling Jewish scribes and Pharisees,
to convince them of my co-operation.
Self-righteous with their scrolls and prophecies,
'Bethlehem, Bethlehem' they muttered hesitantly,
'David's town, for a new shepherd king.
The promised one,
Messiah'.

Was my lavish supper enough
to buy their conspiracy?
'Come back and tell me,
so that I can also worship him.'

The lie slid in with hearty wishes of safe travel,
as hatred seethed within;
my grip ever tightening on my throne.

What if they vanish,
bypassing my murderous ear?
Back-up plans must wield the sword across the region,
eliminate all opposition,
bloodbath in the streets,
even infanticide,
must guarantee my power, kingdom and glory.

No one on earth can stop me.
Taking no chances for history to forget,
my rightful place,
forever in triumph,
eternally lifted up,
'Herod the Great,
King of the Jews.'

Matthew 2:1–18

Alison Stedman is the author of three poetry collections: Raised from
Dust *(2016),* The Song of the Sparrow *(1991) and* Faith Hope
Love *(1987). During her 20 years of nursing, she worked in a London
hospice and lived in Bhutan while serving with The Leprosy Mission. She
now lives on the Isle of Man with her husband, who is a Baptist minister,
and their teenage sons. She is working on her first novel. Her website is www.
alisonstedmanpoetry.com.*

We Should Have Kept Our Eyes on the Star

Carol Purves

THE nights were bitterly cold. In the coolness of the dark, the hot sand of the day felt like frozen salt. Unfortunately, the travelling had to be done at night time; the star was hardly visible in the noonday sky. They were used to this kind of travel, but it was tiring.

Caspar was beginning to feel his age but not willing to give up on this quest. His journey had commenced in the plains of India, though he didn't know how much longer the journey would last or how much more strength he would need to have.

Melchior had journeyed from the rich lands of Persia. His camel was the finest money could buy but his reason for the journey was the same: to find where the star led. His research had told him that it would lead to a new king, a most important king.

Balthazar—still a scholar in his native Babylon—was also following this star. He wanted to be able to worship. They just had to find the place where the birth would take place.

'Now that we've met up, all we need to do is to follow the star. It will lead us to the newborn king.' Caspar was wise as well as learned.

'I'm not so worried about following the star. My charts and study tell me all I need to know.' Balthazar, the youngest, wasn't very experienced.

Melchior just listened and looked on.

Their servants were carrying their precious gifts: gold from the hills of India brought by Caspar, frankincense from gum resin of the trees in Persia from Melchior, and myrrh from the trees of Babylon, the gift from Balthazar. They were worthy gifts for such a great king and they longed for the time when they would be offering them.

Thieves and bandits continually attacked them on the way but they felt safer now that they were travelling together. It must have been obvious that they were carrying great wealth. The cold temperatures at night and the heat of the mid-day sun were also an inconvenience.

After a few more days travelling, Melchior said, 'I think we must be getting near. We've passed into the land of the Israelites.'

'I hope the Romans won't cause us any trouble. I've heard they can be vicious and cruel to strangers.'

'They can be cruel to anyone.' Caspar had heard some frightening stories.

'But then again, I don't think the Jewish people will be any more friendly. Talking about the Romans has given me an idea. Herod is their protector. He's sure to know where this baby has been born. We should go straight to his palace.' Balthazar was full of so-called good ideas.

'No, I think we should continue following the star. It will lead us to the right place.'

'But to ask Herod would save time.'

Against their wills, Caspar and Melchior let Balthazar direct their route to Herod's palace. Maybe he would know the answer and it would certainly save them time. They'd been on the road for what seemed like ages.

Surprisingly, the meeting with Herod was a pleasant experience. He seemed generally friendly and interested in where they had come from. He appeared most anxious to know more about this baby king.

'I've consulted my astrologers, and they tell me the baby will be born in Bethlehem,' he told them. Would they return and let him know where the baby could be found so that he could worship him also?

It seemed they hadn't really saved time, so they went back

following the star as it headed towards Bethlehem. How amazed they were when it stopped, not in front of a palace or mansion, but over a lowly stable in the tiny village. Inside they found others worshipping the baby: shepherds and the townsfolk, the inn keeper and his wife, herdsmen and interested villagers. Never had a journey ended in such a way, but there was no doubt that this cooing little baby was the king whom they were seeking.

They were delighted to offer their gifts. The baby continued cooing while the parents looked on proudly, amazement registering on their faces. They'd never even seen gold, frankincense or myrrh before.

The wise men left the stable intent on returning to Herod. However, the next morning they were amazed that in the night they each had had an identical dream. 'Return home another way.' 'Do not return to Herod.' 'He means to harm the baby.' There could be no doubt about a thrice-dreamed dream. They turned eastwards and continued on their journey.

After a considerable number of days a messenger from Bethlehem caught up with them. He told them, 'Herod was so jealous of this baby king and feared for his kingdom. When you told him about the birth, he ordered the death of all the little boys up to the age of two. Mass murder!'

Stunned, the sages stayed by their caravans, trying to take in the dreadful news.

Ashen and white-faced, Balthazar asked, 'Were all those babies killed because of the news we gave Herod?'

'I think that must have been the case. We thought he was so friendly. He only wanted more information so that this special baby king could be killed.' Melchior was old enough to realise what they had done.

'Killed!'

'Jealous, murdered ...'

'You mean we ...'

'All the babies in Bethlehem ...?'

'We told him ...'

Caspar, a man of few words, could only utter in a strangled voice. 'Those babies died because of us. We should have kept our eyes on the star.'

Carol Purves is the author of four Christian biographies: Gladys Aylward, George Muller, Frances Ridley Havergal and Mary Slessor. She also writes meditations for The Upper Room.

Second Coming

John Thomas

OF course, we three *ourselves* had not made the journey before; but it was—we constantly thought of it—the *second* of such. In truth, we had a good journey (unlike our fathers). The beasts were sure-footed on the sharp stones, the wadis dry with shifting sands, of course, though neither stifling nor too soft; the nights, beyond our furs, not too cold, the stars above guiding true. We, of course, had chosen a better time of year. The inns and caravansaries gladly took our money, sure enough; and nowhere were there scorpions or lice. But when we finally got to the city, things were not quite as we'd expected.

We knew the man Jeshua had perished some years ago—several years, in fact—but word had leaked, and as far as to us, that erstwhile followers swore he still lived. We had travelled in order to ascertain this and, if we might, to see him. Convinced, we were, that his killing had been contrived. Guilt of wrongdoing, we thought, has consequences, rebounds, returns to trouble its doers, and many more besides. Truth was our goal, this was what we sought. Our fathers deserved no less, enfeebled though they now were (though not in mind); and the hopes of coming ages would wish it too.

In many places in the city, we asked about him, the truth about his death. Avoiding rulers, it was the common people we moved among: a beggar sitting by the gates, fallen indigents wracked with pain, poor men, labourers; and many of them we questioned. Quickly we noticed a strange quietude come over them, a reluctance to talk; but the darkness around us, the panic hanging in the air, was everywhere felt by us. Doom and desolation seemed near to all, everyone. I saw it most in the faces, not of supplicants ascending the temple steps, nor costermen crying

in the market-places, but of the actual soldiers themselves—
Romans, of course; 'twas as if they had some inside knowledge
of how all here would end. Then it was, walking in a smaller
street, perhaps asking a woman or workman about his death, that
a rough, calloused hand dragged us into a dark by-way beside
stables and byres. 'I know a man ... who follows his Way ... said
to be a tentmaker; says he's surely still alive. In fact, the man's just
returned to the city ... always moving though, travelling ... I can
take you to him ... with a little ... aid ...'

We duly paid him, and thus, we came to sit at the strange
man's feet. Behind, beyond, the water of his eyes, shone a fire
fed with no earthly fuel. 'Alive? See him?' he said. 'Yes ... oh yes!
And, there are three of you, and thus three gifts I will give to you.
Firstly, for every man—and yourselves, I hope—I give a gift that
may last you all your days, to go with you through the dryness of
this world, the desert, the dreary walk of life.'

What, we wondered, would he give us?

'This gift is that, I pray, he may live in your hearts, and never
leave you.'

'And the second?' we urged.

'This, the gift of the present age, while time lasts ...'

But what?

'Why—it is that you have seen him already!'

What?

'Surely! Remember that beggar at the gate, that sick man? That
was Jeshua—and you walked straight past ... Were you looking
for some glorious thing, there and then ... light in-breaking,
perhaps?'

'And the third?'

'Why, that is when we all will have sight of him, when he
comes to us a second time, when those who know him, love him,
will see him, be with him, in eternity. Three gifts, three sightings.
Three, surely, should suffice ... hold them together equally, right-
balanced, and all will come ... Golden crowns, as it might be, will
descend from the true King ...'

We returned unhurriedly to our homelands—high palaces above the plain, gardens watered by deep springs. Only then did I discover where I had seen, before, the tentmaker's gleam—'twas in the eyes of Balthasar, my father (sat, as often, beside the stilled pool raised by a high cistern on the southern, sun-shot terrace) dreaming of the time when he, too, would see the babe again—though not in this world.

John Thomas has written fiction, reviews, drama, and scholarly articles; he self-publishes as Twin Books, www.twinbooks.co.uk. Novels include: Beyond This Wilderness *(2011),* Not Long Now *(2012),* Death Tonight *(2013), and* Aubrey Annersley's Lucky Day *(2016). In 2017 he wrote an Advent carol.*

Fireside Stories

Curl up for a Cosy Read

'Sally Forth'

Colin Taylor

THE old man peered out of his frost-encrusted window and saw a distant figure struggling through the pale cold landscape. Testy, he asked his lad, 'Who's that?' He waggled an irate finger, 'Yonder. My old eyes can't make out who he is. Who is he?'

The boy stared into the falling snow. 'Yes,' he answered. 'I do know who it is. It's Sharon's granddad, collecting kindling wood.'

'He's got a lot to carry. Where does he live? Not too far away, I hope.'

'A long way off, sir,' answered the boy. 'Up at the top of the pass, near the waterfall. Since his wife died, he's lived on his own. His daughter and Sharon, his grand-daughter, worked in your fields last harvest time. Don't you remember?'

The old man didn't remember, but he had got an idea. His eyes had lighted upon the remains of his lunch; ham and chicken, cheeses, bread and fruit. He told the boy, 'Put that lot in a bag; some beer too. Grab your coat and your boots and let's follow him; give him a surprise.'

The old man barked more instructions. 'Get some wood from the log-pile; you carry some and I'll carry the rest.'

Between the wood and the food, they filled four bags. The boy shouldered one bag and picking up the other, found it so weighty it needed both hands. The old man grasped the other two and threw open the outer door. The falling snow swirled around them in dizzying, blinding eddies and the cold air cut deep into their lungs.

The boy complained, 'But it's perishing out!'

'Ignore it. Button your coat up.' The old man was brusque.

'Where's your gloves? How many times have I told you to keep them safe in your coat pocket?'

'Sorry,' mumbled the boy. He'd put his bags down to breathe warmth on his cupped hands.

'What did you say, boy? Speak up.'

'I said sorry, I don't know where my gloves are. I haven't seen them for days.' The sound of flapping arms and slapping hands told he was warming himself.

'We've got to get on. Sling that bag on your back; pick that one up.' The old man was impatient now as he chivvied the lad on. 'Come on. We're going to lose sight of him soon.'

'Sorry.' Pained yelps. The lad had fallen. 'I'm covered in snow.' He wailed, 'It's so hard to walk.' Another plaintive cry, 'I wish I was bigger.'

'Watch for where he's left footprints in the snow. We'll follow them.' A brilliant idea struck the old man, 'I shall put my feet where he put his and you put your feet where mine have been. Watch! This is how you do it. Follow me!' After a few paces, he stopped to check on the boy and saw him struggling yards behind through a deep drift of snow. The old man's voice became gentler, encouraging. 'It's not so hard. You can do it, if you try.' He repeated, 'Put your feet where I put mine.'

'His stride's miles bigger than mine. So's yours. If I have to step that far, I'll fall ....' A gasp and a muffled thud told the old man that the lad had done what he had warned. Fallen again.

'I'm covered in snow. Again,' he wailed.

A gnarled old hand stretched out to take the boy's and a firm but gentle pull lifted him to his feet. They walked on, the boy trying valiantly to keep pace with the old man whilst dashing melting snow from his neck.

The old man asked, 'Can you see him?'

'No,' answered the boy, preoccupied with the dollops of snow down his neck and in his wellies.

'I can't see him either.' A despairing edge to the old man's voice. 'We've lost him. Can't see him in this blizzard.'

'Maybe we can't see him,' the lad informed the old man, 'but I know where he lives. I used to play there with Sharon, when I was young.'

The boy's words made the years rest heavily upon the old man's shoulders. 'Young indeed!'

'It's this way. Follow me,' said the lad, who now led the way. 'We have to cross the stream; it's not wide, but it's pretty deep.' He hadn't quite finished his sentence when there came a splash and a stifled groan. The boy decided on a discreet silence as they moved further into the wood. Under the trees, the snow lay less thickly, and their progress quickened. From the far side of a clearing a distant light beckoned them towards a ramshackle, low-roofed cottage. The old man rapped on its door. His knock didn't ask 'Is anyone in, please let us in', but insisted, 'Open up.'

The door opened and there stood Sharon's granddad. He was astonished as his two visitors stamped the snow off their boots, strode in, and monopolised the meagre fire to warm their frost-reddened hands.

'Here. These are for you,' said the old man, turning to offer the bags he'd lugged along the woodland track. 'The food will be welcome, maybe the wood as well.' He addressed the lad, 'Come on, boy, hand over your two bags.'

The food was indeed welcome, the wood too. Amidst much blushing, confused and stuttered thanks, Christmas toasts were shared.

The old man drew himself up, gained an inch or two in height and sucked an inch or two off his stomach. 'I've not felt so good in years,' he reflected. 'Feel really good. I wonder why?'

A moment longer and the reason dawned, 'Come, lad, come,' King Wenceslas said. 'Let's make some more calls. It's time to sally forth!'

Colin may be a retired teacher and retired Church of England Lay Reader, but he is very much an active scribe, endeavouring to 'write the vision' by offering an inventive and light-hearted insight into familiar texts and tales. He finds the act of writing is a challenging task, but he prays it will continue to be hugely rewarding.

Cara's Christmas

Julia Fursdon

THEY never found the cause of the fire, but the fact remains that Cara found herself and baby Jake standing out in a wet street in pyjamas, watching the flames and smoke enjoying the place she had once called home.

It was a week before Christmas. The woman who normally sorted things at the council had taken annual leave. The boy she saw, when she turned up holding a crying, grubby baby, looked awkwardly down at his notes. Tragedy was so difficult and anyway his job was to deal with housing repairs. He expected they would house her in the New Year. He expected no such thing but what could he say to the frightened young woman in front of him? He told her with absolute confidence, Sharon was on holiday and would be back after Christmas.

Later, a distracted social worker, who checked her phone every three minutes, asked Cara if she could stay with her mother. Relative? Friends? Cara shook her head which would have to do instead of trying to explain Mum lived with her boyfriend in his house, Dad was permanently drunk, likewise her friends who also smoked, took weed and didn't see the point of Christmas. Or Jake for that matter. The social worker's tired face clouded. Cutbacks, druggies, old men with alcohol problems, and her in-laws coming for Christmas, crowded her thoughts. And now she had to deal with this. She pointed Cara to an orange plastic bench, while Jake whimpered. There was a Christmas tree in the waiting area, every bauble matching. Christmas carols played over the speaker, angelic choirs with old fashioned words, spilling out beside the drinks machine, where an old man sat, staring into space.

The social worker returned, 'Ok Keira, we've found you a place in a hostel. It's a bit of a hike, but you'll be all right there for a while. The Red Cross will arrange a clothing parcel for you and Jake, it's the best we can do.'

'Cara.'

'What? I've got some paper work to do then I'll take you.'

The hostel was nearly an hour away, in a place Cara had never been to. There was a row of shops, bravely decorated for the season, a church, a couple of houses and then a shady garden with a notice, 'Gloucester House'.

The social worker hurried them out of the car, unstrapping the baby and handing him to Cara, without speaking to either of them. She rushed through the front door and into the hall, calling, 'Marion, I've brought that girl and her baby we were talking about.'

Marion stared at them resentfully.

'Look, I've got to dash. It's a nightmare this time of year.' And with that, the social worker left.

'You're in room five, Keira,' Marion told her, walking ahead of her up the stairs. 'I'll give you a key and you mustn't lose it, OK? That's very important, do you understand?'

Cara nodded. Marion opened the door and left. Cara closed the door and let the quiet surround her while she looked at the room. The walls were painted lilac. There was just room for a double bed and a rickety cot. Somebody still knew how to find orange bedspreads. There was a sink, a shower and an empty wardrobe.

Cara changed Jake's nappy, fed him, and wrapped him in an old t-shirt. Then she lay on the bed, and stared at the ceiling, as if an answer might appear among the dust and cracks. She nearly fell asleep, because boredom and not eating turn out to be very tiring. But Jake began to whimper, and Cara felt that knot of fear that had been with her for so long tighten in her stomach. The feeling that any moment she would fall off the edge of the world. She began to hum. What was it? The tune of a Christmas carol, one they had been playing earlier, she thought. 'Away in a manger'? How did the words go? 'Away in a manger, no crib for a bed, the little Lord Jesus lay down His sweet head.' As she sang, she found she remembered the words. She was singing the words she'd learned at primary school to her own baby.

Long ago, in primary school, Cara had been chosen to be Mary. She remembered the envy of the other girls, and the blue veil made her feel special. She rocked Jake on her lap, remembering it all from so long ago. Finally, Jake fell asleep. Cara let him lie beside her on the bed, as the winter light darkened, changing the colours of the room to browns and greys. She lay on the bed and let the Christmas story play in her head: the Angel calling Mary, Mary being afraid and the Angel saying not to be afraid. Joseph, the trip to Bethlehem and no room at the inn for baby Jesus, Saviour of the world. He was only a doll, of course, but for a moment Cara had loved him, so tiny and brave and so far from home. What did it mean to be Saviour of the world? Did that include everyone? Her mum with her bleached hair, Mick with his 'how long are you going to be here?' look, her dad, bottle in hand, staring at the telly, her friends laughing at her for being silly enough to keep Jake? Did that include her? She looked down at Jake, a baby like Jesus. How could a baby be anyone's saviour? Cara didn't know. Outside in the street, she could hear more carols, real people singing this time. Carefully, she put Jake in the cot, went to the window and looked out at the street. She watched until she undressed and got into bed. It was dark now and Cara drifted off. In her dream, she thought she saw an angel with a bright light that dazzled. She turned her face away, but the angel touched her with his soft wings and said, 'Do not be afraid, Cara, I bring you glad tidings of great joy. To you a Saviour has been born, you will find him.'

Julia Fursdon is a member of Stowmarket Wordsmiths which inspires her to write. She has five grown-up children, two dachshunds and has self-published a novel: The Prairie Patchwork.

An Ordinary Sheep

Karen Rosario Ingerslev

I DON'T want to be a sheep. I want to be Mary, or at the very least an angel—perhaps the Angel Gabriel, although Miss Cooper has renamed him the Angel Gabrielle and I'm not sure of the theological implications of that. Sophie Brightside has been cast as Mary. Sophie has blue eyes and very blonde hair. I'm not sure of the theological implications of that either.

My eyes are brown, and my hair is very dark. I was sure I was in with a chance at being cast as Mary. I grew my hair long in preparation and I was going to sing *Mary's Boy Child* at the audition. But Miss Cooper never called an audition. She just announced our parts. And, sure, I might come across as a little timid in class and I don't shout as loudly as Sophie in the playground. But that doesn't mean I'm ok with being a sheep. I've got socks on my hands and cotton wool in my hair and I'm wearing my brother's old pyjamas. The angels have pretty dresses and wings and Mary gets to wear a cape. A dazzling blue cape with a superhero's logo on the underside. Don't even get me started on the theological implications of *that*.

We're thirty seconds in and already there's an emergency. Harry Jackson who's playing Joseph has lost his special green crayon. Harry can't go onstage (or anywhere for that matter) without his special green crayon. Tears are streaming down his face as Miss Cooper coaxes (no, *begs*) him to go on. If Joseph or Mary or Gabrielle won't perform, all of heaven and earth will wait till they are ready. If a sheep were to fall down a well and miss their entrance nobody would even notice. There are hundreds of sheep and you don't need to be anybody special to play one. There is only one Mary and it takes somebody very special to be picked for such a task. That somebody special is

Sophie Brightside. She marches onstage, indifferent to Harry's tantrum, her cape billowing menacingly behind her. The audience coo and wave and take photos.

From my little bench at the side, I try to be the best sheep I can be, but nobody is paying me any attention. Even my own mother is busy taking a photo of Sophie Brightside. You can already tell that she is going to play Mary her entire life, whilst I am forever destined to be a sheep.

A substitute crayon has been found for Harry and he shuffles onstage. He stares at his feet through the entire performance, his resentment for the limelight as great as my hunger for it.

Suddenly it's my scene and I trot onstage with the four shepherds and the seven other sheep. I scamper a little hurriedly to my position and strike a pose. The pose of *curious sheep number eight*. I watch my mum craning her neck to count all the sheep. She finally spots me and waves. Sophie Brightside's mother is sat next to her. They whisper something to each other. Probably something about how wonderful Sophie is. Then they share a chuckle. Probably at my cotton wool hat.

The chorus of angels glide gracefully across the hall looking like a delicate throng of, well ... *angels*. They have glitter in their hair and tinsel round their wrists and prettiest of them all is Poppy Prim, the Angel Gabrielle. *I wish I was pretty enough to be an angel.*

We make our way to the stable. It isn't a real stable, of course. It's actually just two chairs. There is only enough room for Mary and Joseph, so I sit on the floor with the rest of the sheep, trying to get into character as I peer at the special baby in Mary's lap.

What should a sheep do in this moment? I wonder.

I move a little too awkwardly and, as I lean in, Sophie Brightside waves the baby Jesus in the air and accidentally rams his foot up my nose. I stumble backwards and clutch my face, waves of pain mingled with self-pity.

The three kings make their entrance and I yawn loudly. This bit isn't theologically accurate either and I silently appeal for someone, anyone, to step in. But nobody does. Not even Mrs Turner from Sunday School and she's usually the worst for accuracy. Everybody just cheers. As if it's all a game. As if it is not emotionally scarring to be typecast as a sheep so early on in my life. One of the kings sits right in front of me, obscuring me completely. I try to give him a friendly nudge to get him to move but he doesn't take the hint.

We stand for the final song and I sing as loudly as I can in the hopes that Miss Cooper registers even a little bit of remorse at not giving me a better role. There is always the Easter show. Another shot at another Mary.

I take my bow somewhat coyly, aware that nobody in their right mind will be cheering for the sheep, except for my mum who has finally remembered to take my photo. The angels step forward and do a twirl. Harry Jackson has lost his green crayon again and is inconsolable through his and Sophie's bow.

In all the commotion, the baby Jesus (a *girl* doll, by the way) has been discarded face down on the floor. I'm not meant to touch Jesus because I'm just a dirty sheep, but when nobody is looking I gingerly pick him up and slide him back into the manger.

The show is over and it's time for Maths. I pull off my cotton wool hat and shuffle off the stage. I shall never be Mary or an angel or anybody extraordinary.

I take one last glance at the manger.

Oh Lord Jesus, have mercy on me, an ordinary sheep.

Karen Rosario Ingerslev is the writer of the Livi Starling *books, a very British coming-to-faith teen series. She could also tell a tale or two from the three years she and her husband spent living out of suitcases as they followed Jesus through more than forty different cities (including Jerusalem, Fort Mill, Toronto, Cardiff and London) and the trials and treasures they discovered when their faith was put to the test.*

The Wish Bone

Margaret Gregory

IT was after Mom and I left America and came to England that I started going to school. At first, in September, I was too shy to talk to the other children and no one noticed me. It was later that they started gathering round in the playground and making fun of me.

When the dinner bell rang, after one specially bad playtime, I ran out of school, all the way up the hill, past the corner sweet shop, without stopping, and straight into my grandparents' tall quiet house.

After dinner I helped Grandma wash up. Mom was lying down with a sick headache, so I told Grandma instead.

'The children say I talk funny and, if I'm a girl, why do I wear boys' boots?' I sobbed.

'I never did like those Shirley Temple type boots,' Grandma sniffed, 'good enough for Milwaukee, I suppose.'

'And the children say I look like a teddy bear in my furry coat!'

'We'll put a stop to that, Lucy, m'duck, don't you worry!' Grandma said loudly.

The next Saturday Grandma took me into Leicester High Street and bit by bit she turned me into a complete English schoolgirl. I had a new black velour hat, a dark blue winter coat and, very best of all, black shoes with cross-over bars.

Now back home I danced in front of her long wardrobe mirror in all my new clothes, singing, 'Thank you, dear Grandma, thank you!'

I showed them to Mom too. 'No more teddy bear coat for me!'

'It's a perfectly good coat!' she said a little crossly, putting it in her bedroom cupboard. 'Expensive too.' She sighed. 'We don't have that sort of money now, honey.'

For a moment my new clothes were forgotten and I was back in that place where all my hurtful thoughts were like having to give up the big toys I couldn't bring on the boat to England, and the very worst of all: saying goodbye to Daddy.

But at school everything seemed to get better after I started wearing my new winter outfit. The weeks passed and in class we were getting very excited about the Christmas pantomime our teacher was practising with us and the bigger children. It was called 'Cinderella' and I was to be a page like my best friend, Mary Molloy. As Christmas drew nearer, I tried to remember about Christmas in America, but I only had a picture of my Daddy struggling to get a giant Christmas tree through the doorway of our apartment. I'd started to cry because I thought the tree would be taken away. But Daddy just cut off the very top branches and brought it into a corner of our sitting room and I helped to decorate it.

On the Friday evening after we broke up for the Christmas holidays, Grandma and I sat cleaning the silver at the kitchen table.

'I've got a surprise for you, Lucy! I'm taking you to see Father Christmas tomorrow!'

'Oh, Grandma!' I ran around to kiss her, even though my fingers were dirty from the silver polish. 'Will he give me a present?'

'We must wait and see.'

I could hardly get to bed quickly enough that night! I longed to meet Father Christmas and maybe get a present. Mom had warned me not to expect many presents that year, with Daddy in America, still trying to find work.

Saturday came at last. After waiting in line with Grandma and many other children in Leicester's biggest shop I entered Father Christmas's snowy, sparkly grotto. Would I get a present?

'Have you been a good girl?' he asked, his long white beard

wobbling up and down as he spoke. I didn't like giving up half my Saturday penny in chapel on Sundays, I remembered. But would that really count?

'Most days,' I said.

Father Christmas laughed and I watched his hand draw out of his sack a doll with rosy cheeks and golden curls. My lovely present!

And there were lots of other good things to follow as my first Christmas in England drew nearer. Grandma let me help make lemon curd tarts and mince pies—I'd never tasted them before—and, best of all, ice a huge Christmas cake. I went to bed extra early on Christmas Eve.

'Do you think Father Christmas will find me now we live in Leicester and not Milwaukee?' I asked Mom as we hung up a very long sock on the bed post.

'Oh, he'll make it!' Mom assured me.

I lay awake in my shadowy attic bedroom, listening to the wind blowing amongst the big trees in the park opposite. Or maybe it was the whirr of Father Christmas's sleigh? I listened and listened.

Suddenly it was morning time and even before I scrambled out of bed I could see my long sock bulging out on all sides.

The morning passed quickly as I played with my new toys and very soon Mom was calling, 'Lucy, wash hands and come to the table!'

It was only after I'd eaten my first English turkey dinner with sausages and stuffing that Grandma cried out, 'We've forgotten the wish bone! That'll never do! Grandpa, you and Lucy can pull it.'

We each held a leg of this strange little V-shaped bone.

'Make a secret wish, Lucy!'

I closed my eyes tight and pulled. Then a strange thing happened. All the presents and excitement of Christmas faded away. I was back in that hurtful place where the only thing I wanted was for Daddy to be with us. I squeezed my eyes tighter to hold in the tears. There was a little crack. 'You've got the bigger bit of wish bone, Lucy,' Grandpa was saying.

Grandma carried in the Christmas pudding. Mom wiped my cheek as she went into the kitchen. Her eyes looked watery too, I thought, but she whispered, smiling, 'Who's my brave girl then?'

Margaret Gregory, a former foreign language student, has had a lifelong interest in words and writing. Her earlier work included general stories for children and for Sunday-School teaching, and adult articles, which used the encouraging opportunities offered by church magazines.

Christmas Cameo

Marion Andrews

'BIG issue; Big issue?'

The last shoppers hurried past. The rain soaked through her thin anorak, making her long dark hair twinkle.

'Big Issue?' she tried again 'It's my last copy …'

She sounded desperate and an elderly lady stopped. 'OK I'll have it. It's Christmas and a girl in your condition should be at home, in the warm.'

Mary smiled gratefully. 'Thank you,' adding, 'God bless you.'

Her customer smiled. 'Happy Christmas, Pet. Now you get home.'

Home; Mary sighed. If only it were that simple. It had been once. There had been Mum, Dad, a bed, food, Joe. Her eyes filled with tears as she remembered.

The text message had changed everything. She had been doing homework, in her room, when her phone had bleeped. 'Mary, God has blessed you,' it read. 'You are pregnant. You are to have a child; a boy; you are to call him Jesus.'

Some joke, she thought, scrolling down the screen to identify the caller. Gabriel, it displayed. Who was that? Anyway, she couldn't be pregnant; she was a virgin. She flung the phone down and tried to forget about it, but she didn't delete the message. It filled her with peace; she liked the feeling.

Her parents just stared at her when she told them.

'Pregnant? Oh, Mary, how could you?' her father ranted. 'Wait until I get my hands on Joe.'

'It isn't Joe' she had blurted out, then wept, seeing the horror on their faces. Who could blame them? It was quite a story. Joe's reaction had been similar. He was hurt and didn't know what to do; so he withdrew saying, 'I thought I was "The One", Mary!'

Mary was distraught, so Mum took charge, arranging for her to stay with Auntie Liz, who was also newly pregnant. When Mary left, she felt stronger, more capable.

Back home, Joe visited. She reached for his hand.

'I'm sorry. I didn't want to hurt you. I wish I could explain. I've only ever wanted you!'

He put his finger on her lips. 'It's OK, Babes. I know.' He shrugged. 'I can't explain. I had this dream and now all I want is to care for you and Bump.' He put his hand on her swollen belly and smiled.

The planning began; it seemed they needed to be homeless to get accommodation. So, they had moved into a hostel. Joe had a job making kitchens. Once they had the baby, it seemed they should get a flat!

Back at the hostel, Mary felt bad vibes as she entered. She recognised Joe's raised voice inside the Manager's Office and, hesitantly, knocked on the door. It went quiet, then Rod the manager opened the door. Joe was staring at the floor and didn't respond when Mary asked, 'Joe? What's happening?'

'Are you going to tell her, or shall I?' Joe stared defiantly at Rod.

'Mary, I've explained to Joe,' Rod began. 'This hostel's policy allows people to stay for thirty consecutive nights. You have overstayed this time. Demand is high, and although I'd like to, I can't ignore policy. Rules are rules.'

'What do you mean, Rod?' Mary asked.

Joe snorted. 'He's chucking us out! It's Christmas and we're being thrown out onto the streets to fend for ourselves.' He pushed past Rod and led Mary from the room. 'Happy

Christmas to you too,' he shouted, slamming the office door.

Packing their few belongings into a rucksack they left. Joe looked stern.

'What will we do? Where will we go? What about the baby?' Mary whimpered.

'We'll be ok,' Joe whispered softly. 'There's another hostel, the other side of town. We'll try there.'

Mary sighed. 'But I'm tired, Joe.' She hadn't eaten all day.

Joe took her hand. 'We'll sort out a bed for the night. The other place isn't far! Then we'll get some food.'

The pain, when it came, stopped Mary in her tracks. She clung to a lamp-post unable to speak. Joe held her close, trying to calm the panic that was rising inside.

Mary groaned 'Oh, Joe, I think the baby's coming. What shall we do?' Another pain gripped her.

Joe looked around desperately. A garage with music playing inside was nearby. Joe hammered on the door which was opened by a man in a boiler suit.

'Can you help us, mate?' Joe asked pointing at Mary. 'She's in labour.'

The man, wiping his hands, asked, 'Have you rung an ambulance?' When Joe shook his head, he ran inside. Joe heard him speaking rapidly into his phone, then he shouted, 'Bring her inside. It's warmer.'

Joe took Mary's arm and helped her into the garage. She sank gratefully onto a pile of dust sheets in the corner; the pains were coming regularly now; her body's only mission was to expel the child.

In the semi-darkness, the smell of engines and oil was intoxicating. Her body reacted instinctively. She panted as each pain reached its peak, resting in between contractions. As the mechanic reappeared with some towels and hot water, Mary groaned loudly.

'I've got to push. Baby's coming.' With two pushes the baby slid into the world, objecting lustily to such a rude entrance.

Joe wrapped him in a towel and handed him to Mary saying, 'It's a boy, sweetheart.'

She nodded, tears streaming down her cheeks, and she kissed the child tenderly, whispering, 'Hello, Jesus.'

The room flooded with a strange light, as an ambulance, blue lights flashing, drew up outside. Two young paramedics ran into the garage stopping when they saw the child.

'Think we've missed the main action,' the senior one began, kneeling by Mary. 'But let's have a proper look at you, shall we?'

A motor-bike drew up outside; a pizza delivery driver dismounted and ran into the garage. He looked shocked. 'Tony?' he grinned when his friend appeared. 'You ok? Gave me a fright seeing the ambulance!'

Tony shrugged. 'They just appeared from nowhere; now look, they've got a kid!'

They hugged each other awkwardly. Pizza boy pulled out his phone. 'Just wait until I tell them at Base. A baby born in your garage! Christmas Eve too!'

'And the Word became flesh and dwelt among us, and we have seen His glory.'

Marion Andrews is a Mum/Grandma/Widow/Retired Nurse who writes to satisfy something deep inside. Her novel Angels of the NHS, *published in December 2016, tells the story of the people and experiences she encountered whilst training to be an SRN in London, in the 1960s. It is available on Amazon.*

A Fallen Christmas

Mark Anderson Smith

'DO we have to go?'

'Yes, Emily. We discussed this, remember?'

'But it's Christmas! I haven't opened my presents yet …'

'There will be plenty of time for that later, young woman.'

'Dad!'

Saul turned to his daughter. 'Listen to your mother. Go and put your jacket on.' He watched as Emily glared at him, then stomped out of the living room, the room shaking with every step. 'Are you sure about this,' he whispered to Gloria who was putting the finishing touches on a ribbon, drawing a scissor's edge up the material so that when she let go, it sprang into a curl.

'It will be good for her. Good for us too.' She sighed. 'You've complained the last couple of years that we've lost the meaning of Christmas. If this isn't a way to discover it, I don't know what is.'

'But is it a safe environment for Emily?'

Gloria put down the scissors and raised her hands to her mouth, blowing softly through her fingers as she looked at him. Standing, she stepped towards him and put her hands on his waist.

'We will be with her. God will be with her. I can't think of anywhere that she would be safer.'

He couldn't help but smile. 'You are some woman, Gloria.'

'That I am.' She gave him a kiss.

Emily stomped back into the room, jacket now on, but her buttons done up lopsidedly. 'I want to take a present.'

Saul tried to hide a smile as Gloria rolled her eyes at him. 'She wants to take a present,' he said.

Gloria let go of his waist and turned to Emily, crouching down and unfastening her buttons.

'Young lady, if you want something then you need to ask for it, and you need to be polite and respectful and accept that your parents may have a good reason if they say no.'

One of Emily's feet stamped hard and her face looked as if she was going to either burst into tears or start screaming, but to Saul's surprise she did neither. Instead, her expression softened and her tone was changed when she asked: 'Mummy, can I take a present? Please.'

Gloria didn't answer straight away as she continued refastening the buttons on Emily's coat and fussed with her hair. 'Very well, Emily. You may take one present.'

At once, Emily ran over to the tree and picked up the largest present there.

'I'm hungry, Daddy.'

'I know, honey, but we will get to eat soon.'

'Can I have some turkey?'

'Once everyone else has been fed.'

'But there are so many of them ...'

Saul forced a smile at Emily and continued serving turkey slices to the men and a few women and children in the queue. Emily was right. There were far more people than he had expected. He felt a hand on his arm and looked round to see Tony with a fresh platter of turkey.

'Thanks,' Saul told him. 'Was starting to run out. How many people did you invite?'

Tony laughed as he swapped the platters. 'Everyone.'

'Seriously?'

'Of course. Sent an invite out to every organisation I could think of, inviting people to come, and asking for volunteers.'

'But how did you know we would cope?'

'I didn't. But I trust God will provide. Feeding people seems to be something he enjoys doing.'

Lowering his voice, Saul brought his head closer to Tony's. 'Pity he couldn't have provided more volunteers.'

Nodding thoughtfully, Tony's expression seemed to cloud over for an instant, then his smile returned. He lowered the almost empty platter to Emily. 'Want some turkey?'

She didn't ask Saul for permission, but quickly grabbed a slice and stuffed it in her mouth.

He was about to protest when Tony winked at him.

'Suffer the little children, right?' Clapping a hand on his shoulder, Tony whispered. 'You came. I praise God for that. If Jesus could feed five thousand with one boy's packed lunch and twelve inept disciples, then I think we can manage.'

'Would you like to help Mummy give out the presents,' Saul asked Emily, who was sitting clutching her present, watching her mother intently.

She shook her head.

Saul decided not to push it and instead watched Gloria as she selected presents from the pile under the tree and offered them to people around the room.

'Where are all the other presents?' Emily asked.

'What other presents?'

'Everyone's only getting one present each. Why are they only getting one?'

How did he answer that? That might be one to pass to Gloria later, he was thinking when Emily spoke up again.

'How many presents have I at home?'

'I don't know, we didn't count them.' Definitely a conversation for Gloria to handle.

'She only got one,' Emily said, pointing at a young girl not much older than herself, seated across the room.

'I guess we only bought enough presents to give everyone one,' Saul said.

'It's not enough.'

'Well …' Saul started, but Emily had stood and was now walking across the room, still holding her present. It seemed like everyone's eyes turned towards his daughter.

Emily stopped in front of the other little girl and held out her present. The girl looked up at her mother, her expression questioning.

When the girl didn't immediately take the present, Emily placed it on her lap, leaving the girl little choice but to take hold of it. Turning, Emily then walked back to Saul, a determined expression on her face.

Saul saw Gloria go to Tony and give him the present she was holding, then she also walked over.

'That was a lovely thing to do, Emily,' she said, then wrapped her arms around Emily.

Released from the hug, Emily looked at them both. 'Next year, I want to make cupcakes for everyone.'

Gloria smiled and looked at him. 'What do you think, Saul? Next year, cupcakes?'

He looked round at people who were no longer strangers. 'Sure, why not …'

Mark Anderson Smith's novels include Fallen Warriors, *a thrilling new Christian series that weaves gripping action together with relatable characters in an emotional journey; and* The Great Scottish Land Grab, *a political novel that turned the Scottish independence referendum on its head. Find out more at www.dragonlake.co.uk*

The Uninvited Guest

Michael Limmer

IN the week before Christmas, Bellman—always an enterprising soul—had booked a function room at the biggest hotel in town to host a reunion for as many of Burnaby College's class of '68 as were able to get there.

Matthew Garland went along out of curiosity. He'd kept in touch with a few, Bellman among them, but knew there'd be chaps he hadn't set eyes on since the chapel service on the last day of that long-ago summer term. In a way he'd been looking forward to it. He'd always prided himself on his memory and arrived early, parking himself in an alcove to watch everyone arrive and see if he could put a name to each face. There was only one he couldn't place: a nervous-looking chap in a suit which had seen better days. Try as he might, Garland couldn't recall him to mind.

He made his way through to the bar. It was decked out with paper chains, and a large Christmas tree in the corner was festooned with winking lights of every colour. Everyone seemed in good humour, glasses of bubbly in their hands and party hats on heads, some already worn at a rakish angle, as faces reddened and smiles widened. Garland noticed the stranger chatting to, or rather being chatted at by Bellman. After exchanging greetings with a couple of acquaintances, he managed to draw his old friend aside and asked who the man was.

Bellman laughed heartily. 'Didn't think I'd ever see the day when your memory let you down, Matt. The chap's name's Davison—tells me he was with us for a few terms round about the third and fourth years.' Bellman went on his merry way, leaving Garland unconvinced. He caught up with the stranger at the first opportunity.

'It's Davison, isn't it? I'm Matthew Garland. Let me see now. You were at Burnaby in the fourth year?'

'I left halfway through it.' The man's gentle voice matched his unassuming features. 'My parents moved up north.'

'I see.' Garland shepherded Davison away from the crowd, uncomfortable with what he was about to say. 'My friend, I have a very good memory for names and faces. But I can't seem to place yours.' He wondered uneasily if the man might say he'd been at Burnaby sometime after Garland had left, that he'd seen Bellman's blurb in the newspaper and had mistaken the year. But immediately Davison's shoulders slumped, and his gaze was cast down to the floor.

'You shouldn't be here, should you?' Garland's voice was tinged with pity.

Davison smiled sadly and set down his half-empty glass. 'I'm sorry. I'd better leave.' He turned and walked from the room, just as dinner was announced.

Oblivious to the stampede for the dining-room, Garland watched him depart. He regretted his interference, for he saw a man perhaps down on his luck seizing the chance of a free meal.

'Aren't you coming in, Matt?' Bellman was frowning at him.

'In a moment, Tom.' Almost without knowing what motivated him, Garland rushed out into the foyer. 'I say—wait! Please—wait!'

He caught up with the startled Davison as he was on the point of leaving the hotel.

'Listen, as it's Christmas, I—well, I'd be more than happy to stand you this meal. Please—do stay. As my guest.'

A slow smile lit up Davison's face, and his voice wavered as he replied. 'Thank you. You're very kind.'

They returned to the dining-room. 'Let me introduce Davison,' Garland announced to his neighbours as they took their seats. 'He was only with us for a few terms ...'

Everyone moved around between courses, and Garland's last glimpse of Davison was of him shyly conversing with the group at his table. There was a contented air about him, as if he felt he was among friends. Garland missed him over coffee and asked Bellman if he'd seen him.

'He's just left. Charming fellow, and full of praise for you. You remembered him eventually, then?'

'Oh yes. Memory's definitely at fault. Must be age, you know.'

Garland went out into the foyer to find Davison gone. However, a note had been left for him at reception. Curious, Garland opened it. On a sheet of hotel notepaper was written the one sentence: *I was a stranger, and you took me in.*

'Yes,' Garland murmured. 'I suppose I did.'

He returned to the celebrations filled with a joy surpassing the effects of the good food and wine. He wondered if he might have received a timely reminder of what Christmas was really about.

Michael Limmer spent thirty-two years as a bookseller and bookshop manager, and a further thirteen running the book department at a local garden centre. He has written three full-length mystery thrillers, as well as publishing collections of his stories and poems and a wide range of Christian greetings cards on behalf of three Christian charities.

The Gift Unwrapped

Ren Smith

I DON'T recall when it arrived. Delivered by hand perhaps or by that smiling postie who, remarkably often, seems to distribute post around the village with very little reference to the actual address for which it was intended. As this results in a game of swapping and redistribution I quite likely thought it possible that the parcel was not meant for me at all. Although now I am sure that it was.

Perhaps I put it aside, thinking I would give it some attention when I had a bit of time, which of course I never did have and so, well, it got forgotten. Laid aside, it started that insidious journey such items seem to take; from the kitchen table to the dresser, from the dresser to the desk in the back room, from the desk to the junk cupboard.

'Just for now, of course, while we have visitors.'

Inevitably, a time when I would sort it out, see it on its way to its proper destination and intended function, is lost somehow in the heave and heartiness of the season.

It is forgotten. Time passes. Dust accumulates. The gift waits.

Several Christmases pass by until this latest one. Yet again I heave the box of decorations out of the cupboard. Some hours later the downstairs rooms are transformed into a grotto of glitter and sparkle. Only one thing is missing. The lights, draped around the little artificial tree we drag out each year, have had enough. They have died and no tedious replacement of fiddly little bulbs is going to resuscitate them. Impatiently I drag things out of the cupboard. Surely I have some more lights somewhere. I'm just about to give up and stuff everything back in when my hand brushes against the neglected gift at the very back of the shelf. I bring it out into the grey December light and for the first time study it properly. Its wrapping is scuffed and torn, the label faded beyond deciphering.

A quiet, gentle whisper seems to quiver in the air.

'Why have you not opened me?'

'I really do not know,' I whisper back.

I carefully peel off the wrapping to reveal a small box made from old Christmas cards. Every side pictures the Nativity. Jesus is a black baby, a white baby, a brown baby. He is well nourished and plump, he is thin and underweight, he is a newborn lying in his mother's arms, he is a toddler sitting on her knee. He is every baby, held in the bosom of families of every nation on Earth. It is a beautiful work of creativity and I wish I had opened it earlier, right at the beginning when I first received it.

Carefully removing the lid, I look inside for what I am certain will be something wonderful. The box is empty. Disappointment is an almost physical sensation, somewhere near my heart. But now I can see, almost invisible against the plain lining of the box, a piece of tightly folded paper. Slowly, carefully, I unfold it and see, written in faded but exquisite script, the following verse:

'This little box is full of love
Which, like the wind, cannot be seen.
And yet it's true that where love dwells
It clearly shows where love has been.
Receive this blessing. Pass it on
And even when the box has gone
The Gift remains. God's Gift to you
His Love to nourish all you do.'

When had I received this gift? Who had sent it? Why had I not opened it at the time?

How often do we receive God's precious gift, even say 'thank you', but still leave the Gift unwrapped, unexplored and unused?

Loving and gracious Father, as we approach this season of remembering the birth of your Son, please help us to see through the dross and commercialism, to resist the overindulgence and greed and to see your wonderful Gift to us as He really is. Help us to unpack the true meaning of His birth and to live our lives in the light of that knowledge.

Ren Smith has been a rebellious teenage child of our Father for years and years and years. She lives on the Norfolk coast, writes poetry and 'stuff' and is somehow put up with by her spouse, Bar, and their lurcher, Gideon.

A Modern Samuel

Rosemary Johnson

'For this child I prayed, and the Lord has granted me my petition that I made to him. Therefore I have lent him to the Lord. As long as he lives, he is lent to the Lord.'

1 Samuel 1:27–28

DAVE is eating the sausage rolls as I take them out the oven.

'Leave some for Sam.' I smack his hand.

'Sam's not back until Boxing Day. Am I not allowed to eat anything until then?'

I shrug. On my feet in the kitchen since first thing this morning, every bone in my body throbs with exhaustion. I love doing the traditional baking on Christmas Eve—Christmas cake, Christmas pudding, mince pies, trifle, turkey, brandy sauce, sausage rolls—usually.

His mouth full of soft, friable sausage roll, Dave lays his hand on my shoulder. 'Don't be sad, love. I expect he's having the time of his life.'

I bang baking trays into the sink, enjoying the clanging of metal on stainless steel. 'Yeah. I know.'

He helps himself to a mince pie. 'Anyway, I'm off to church. Choir practice. You coming to Crib Service this afternoon?'

The first time I ever took Sam to church, nine years ago, was for Crib Service. I was so proud of the tiny, sleeping, bundle in my arms, the answer to prayer, not just mine, or Dave's, but of everyone at church.

Yet we've sent him away.

'I've got to decorate the trifle.'

Dave's better at fending off the comments than I am.

'I could never leave my child at boarding school,' Carol, our churchwarden, once said. 'Even a choir school.'

This afternoon it'll be, 'Isn't Sam home yet? It's Christmas.' And: 'I expect he'll be singing in services at the cathedral.'

'Well, no.' Maybe I'll feel different when he does, but Sam's a Deputy Singing Boy, not a full member of the cathedral choir— yet.

'And why aren't you at the cathedral with him?'

Even harder to explain is that Dr Tuffen, the choir master, encourages parents to stay away from Christmas services, until Boxing Day.

The phone rings as the noise of Dave's car engine fades into the distance.

'Mummy!'

'Hello darling.'

'Mummy …' He draws in an enormous breath. Years ago, I stood by his cot watching his chest moving up and down to reassure myself he was breathing. '… Ben Avery's got a sore throat.'

'Poor Ben.' Ben Avery was one of the senior choristers.

'Geddit, Mummy, geddit.'

A choir-school mother for twelve months, I geddit all right.

'Harry or me has got to sing this afternoon.'

Harry is the other Deputy Singing Boy.

'Darling … don't be too disappointed if it's Harry.'

'Harry was eating peanut butter at breakfast. Everybody knows that peanut butter makes you not able to sing.'

I skip back into the kitchen after he's rung off. Must get cream on trifle. Wouldn't it be amazing beyond anything if Sam made his choir debut at the Nine Lessons and Carols on Christmas Eve? Very disappointing for Ben, of course, and his parents. I mustn't be like Harry's mother, Janey. Right on cue, a text message flashes up on my phone—from Janey. 'Have you heard? So excited.'

I think about how to reply, but, in the end, I don't. Whatever is that dreadful noise? It's the cream beating away in the food processor and forming itself into solid, buttery peaks.

Every Saturday and every Sunday, we travel up to London to hear Evensong at the cathedral, craning our necks—attempting not to appear to do so—as the choir processes in, hoping, longing, to see our boy's fair head amongst the deep blue cassocks and white surplices. Afterwards, we take Sam out, often to Lillywhites in Piccadilly Circus, where we drool over football kits. We've bought Sam the Arsenal home strip for Christmas. Cost us a mint, but he's our boy. Afterwards, we eat pizza, hot, greasy, salty, and inexpensive—nine-year-old heaven. We watch him gobbling up slice after slice, making ourselves believe that these few hours will never end. Later, saying goodbye in the dormitory is agony. He's never cried, although I do, frequently, in the car on the way home.

'He's fine. He's enjoying it,' Dave tells me, at different points along the motorway.

What's amazed me is how soon Sam became engulfed in choir-school, telling musical jokes, working out which football team every choir-school boy supports, and charting his way up the singing ladder. I do hope he's not too disappointed this afternoon, because—I hate to admit this—Harry's a better singer than Sam. Janey was taking him to junior opera workshops in the West End when he was fresh out of nappies, whereas Sam's previous musical experience is limited to singing in our own church choir. Janey is pushy. Rumour has it she asked Dr Tuffen, the choir director, if Harry could sing a solo at the school concert, and he did, terrifyingly well.

I do go to Crib Service. I can't bear the wondering and waiting at home.

The phone's ringing as I open the front door on my return.

'Mummy, we sang. We really did sing.'

'What? Oh darling, that's wonderful. Er ... we?'

'Yeah. It was a bit of a squash in the choir stalls, but Harry and I are quite thin.'

183

'Wish we'd seen you.'

''S all right, Mummy. I'll sing again. Soon. Dr Tuffen says parents are a distraction at Christmas.'

'No Ben still?' says Carol the Churchwarden, handing me my service-book at Midnight Mass.

'No, he's needed. At the cathedral.'

As you listen to carols and Christmas music, spare a thought and a prayer for choirboys and choirgirls at cathedrals, abbeys and Oxbridge colleges. Aged nine to thirteen, they rehearse every day and sing, as equals, alongside adult professional singers. Many of them spend Christmas Day at boarding school.

Rosemary Johnson has published short stories in Every Day Fiction, Mslexia, Alfie Dog Fiction, The Copperfield Review *and* Circa. *She blogs about writing and everyday life at* Write On. *In real life, Rosemary lives with her husband and cat in Essex and, despite having attempted to retire once, still teaches information technology.*

Cowshed to Kitchen

Trevor Stubbs

WIND *and rain again!* Tom sighed to himself as he trudged through the mud on his way to the cowshed long before dawn. With the clouds as they were, on the shortest day of the year it was hardly worth the sun bothering. The cows were pleased to see Tom—even if they weren't going into the fields, at least the discomfort of their udders would be addressed, and the hay and silage smelt good.

It was as the beasts were making their way through the yard, that he spotted him. Tom wasn't surprised. The warmth of a cowshed was always welcome to wayfarers on their way through. But Tom needed to get rid of him. The farmer wasn't mean, but a cowshed was not a safe place to have 'men of the road' that often brought a lethal combination of meths and matches into their bed of straw.

'Oi, on your way!' called Tom.

'I come to see the baby,' replied the tramp.

'What baby?'

'The one the angels told me about just as I was leaving the Cat and Fiddle.'

'You've got the wrong place. Nothing but cows in this shed. Anyway, if Jesus were here, I don't think he would want to see you. You're not a shepherd and you are certainly not a king; what you are is worse for wear. Sorry, mate, I can't let you stay here. Health and safety.'

'But it's pissing down, mate.'

'I know it is,' answered Tom as he thought of a second reason why having guests in a cowshed without *en suite* facilities wasn't a good idea. 'But a cowshed isn't for human beings.'

'It were for Jesus!'

Tom thought fast. 'Th—that was by arrangement—for one night only,' he stammered.

'I tried ringing your door bell, but you weren't at home. So I had to just come … What happened to Jesus on the second night?' the wayfarer asked.

'No idea.'

'Bet they didn't turf Jesus out into the wind and the rain.' The tramp resumed his seat on a bail of straw and began rolling a ciggy. He coughed alarmingly.

'You can't light up in here!' exclaimed the farmer. 'Oh, all right. You can come into the kitchen and have some tea and a sandwich. But you must promise not to light that thing in the house—we've got a baby.'

'Told you I's come to see the new baby.'

By the time Tom had finished the milking, the wayfarer had consumed a large breakfast provide by Tom's wife, Lynn, and was cooing over his little daughter. Tom shuddered, but the little girl appeared besotted with her new admirer.

'Can you give Frank a lift to the friary?' asked Lynn. 'He's due there for Christmas.'

Tom readily agreed. The inconvenience of an hour's return journey would be worth it to get Frank well off the premises.

Five years later, the Christmas weather was exactly the same. Wind and rain—it hardly did anything else at Christmas. This year the river was so high it was threatening to burst its banks. Tom did his work in the dairy as he always did, looking forward to the warmth and welcome of his kitchen where he now had two more children to add to his little girl. He pushed open the door to see a man in the visibility jacket of the environment agency. He looked vaguely familiar.

'Hello,' said the man. 'I'm here to help with the river. But I wanted to pop by to say thank you for saving my life five years ago.'

'Saved your life?' queried Tom.

'Yeah. I'm Frank. You took me in, you remember? I came

looking for a baby and an angel, and I found them in this kitchen. If you hadn't taken me to the friary that day, I would have died on the road. I had the beginnings of pneumonia and they had to rush me to hospital the next day. They cleaned me up and got me through. I got to thinking of the way your baby smiled at me—the first real smile anyone gave me in years. It was the beginning—a light in the darkness.

'I've kicked the booze and have been working for the past four years. When we repaired the wall down the valley, a bloke called *me* an angel, and I thought of you and your wife … and your baby again … She'll be five now. I've brought this for her.'

Over another large farm breakfast, Frank gave the girl a baby doll.

'Thank you,' she said. 'This is my first Christmas present! Are you Father Christmas not dressed up, or a hangel without wings?'

The workman shrugged.

'What's baby's name? He's like baby Jesus,' asked the girl, wrapping the doll in his blanket.

'You can call him Jesus, if you like, but don't leave him in the cowshed. Make sure you bring him into the kitchen. He belongs inside with you.'

'Course,' said the child, emphatically. 'Jesus was borned outside but they didn't leave him there, did they?'

Trevor Stubbs, now retired from full-time ordained ministry in various parts of the world, divides his time between youth work, supporting theological education in South Sudan and writing. His published works include the four books of the White Gates Adventures series, which he describes as 'fantasy fiction with a spiritual heart', for young adults and anyone who enjoys reading stories about young people.

Jesus is Here

Veronica Bright

THE river is held in the first light of the day. A mist haunts the water and a heron stands motionless. The abbot inhales the scent of wet grass and leaves that are returning slowly to the soil. This is the place where he feels closest to God, where he comes to renew his inspiration.

He sighs. All has not been going well at the monastery for some time. Take the gardener monks, for example. The tool shed is a mess, and only this week the abbot came across a couple of forks left out in the rain. The cooks are no better. Yesterday they burnt the potato and onion soup, and there were lumps in the custard as big as hailstones. Even Brother Thomas, once so reliable, has recently let the chickens escape among the cabbages, and by the time he and another monk had rounded them up and driven them back into their pen, the succulent leaves were laced with holes. How could this brother, named after Thomas of Canterbury for his diligence, have grown so careless?

The abbot rubs his hands to warm them. He has admonished, albeit gently, the culprits. He has tried to encourage them in the monastic life. He believes that appreciation works better than reproach.

A small flock of birds rises from a field across the river, black wings flapping loosely to reveal pure white. Eee-ooo-eeep, they cry, as if longing for help. Lapwings. The abbot names them silently. Then he turns and walks thoughtfully back to the monastery buildings. Perhaps it is the onset of winter that is affecting the monks. As soon as Advent began, there were mornings of stiff frost and, with these, came a reminder that the harsher side of life must now be borne. In two weeks it will be Christmas, but how can they celebrate the joy of Christ's birth if they are all weighed down with cold, and weary with enduring?

Has the abbot not reassured the monks enough? He has told them that Advent is a time of preparation, that Jesus is coming, that there is hope. Is it that the brothers are not going to bother until He arrives? Or perhaps, he thinks, ever seeking the charitable explanation, they are saving the best until He comes. He can only pray about the situation and try to be patient; for, surely, grumbling will only make his dear brothers worse.

The next day, as the abbot is being served with a portion of rather dubious-looking soup, he looks at the monks as they sit at their refectory tables. His glance goes from bowed head to bowed head. 'Jesus is here,' he whispers. He believes it. It is simply a matter of convincing the men in his care.

The monk who has brought the soup takes his place on a wooden bench. After the meal, in the kitchen, he whispers to the cook. 'Jesus is here. I heard the abbot say it.' The cook's eyes open a little wider. Later the cook whispers to the monk who is fetching water from the well. 'Jesus is here.'

The next day there are more whispers. The brothers begin to look around. If Jesus is here, they want to see Him, to meet Him. They keep their eyes open in the garden. There is no stranger there. They take furtive peeps in the chapel. There is no stranger here. They look around the laundry. Still no stranger.

On the Sunday before Christmas, the monks are allowed a time of brotherhood. They exchange talk. One of the oldest monks says, 'If Jesus is already here, perhaps He's one of us.'

The abbot meanwhile has not ceased to pray. As the days take them all towards the Saviour's birth, he notices something. The gardeners clean their tools and hang them up in their allotted places. The cooks use the same ingredients, but the meals are tastier. Nothing is burnt and there is not a lump to be found in the custard. There is an air of cheerfulness and compassion throughout the monastery. Brother helps brother. Expressions soften. Eyes shine.

On Christmas Day the dawn is late and wintry. Yet there is

something golden about it. In the chapel the abbot stands to address his fellow monks. Today their attention is wholly focussed on him.

'My brothers,' he says, 'we are here to celebrate our Saviour's birth a little over one thousand one hundred years ago.' There is a long silence as he rests kind eyes on each man in turn. 'Jesus is here,' he says. 'Each one of you has brought Him here. Long may He stay.'

Veronica Bright has won over forty prizes for her short fiction, but the art of producing a good novel has so far eluded her. She gets a monthly boost from fellow members of the Plymouth Christian Writers Group, which she runs, and she seeks to be encouraging in her role as the short story adviser for the Association of Christian Writers. www.veronicabright.co.uk

I Wonder as I Wander

Seasonal Memories and Musings

The Snowman

Eirene Palmer

CAN Christians be selfish? The popular view of Christians, or people who go to church, is of selfless saints who work their fingers tirelessly to the bone for the good of others, never giving a thought to their own needs and desires, casting off their shirt from their back to the beggar in the street, giving their last crust to a starving dog. Oh, you know what I mean, you get the drift. Christians are not supposed to be selfish.

Well, last Christmas I felt selfish. We have a large blended family of six kids—a glorious mish-mash of ages, sexes, situations, partners, needs, anxieties and demands. And they descend at Christmas bringing all their baggage with them, literally and metaphorically. We ask them to deposit the literal stuff in the garage so it's well out of the way—but they usually forget, and we spend two weeks breaking our necks on rucksacks left on the kitchen floor. But we love them all beyond words, as you do your kids, and we would do anything for them. We like to give them a break. They all work hard, very hard because life in today's working world isn't easy—a decision we both came to a couple of years ago, opting out with early retirement. But we both had the benefit of a baby-boomer pension pot and a paid-up mortgage which to our kids seems like the end of the rainbow.

So, we aim to give them a good time and a rest when they come back. We cook, we clean, we open up the bar in the garage and generally let them revert to being seven again. (Not that our seven-year olds were helping themselves from a bar, I hasten to add). And we don't mind. We really don't. They'll choose our care home one day.

Until that last morning. After a late night playing a keenly fought contest of pub games between seven of us, we parents rose early and cooked a full English to sustain them. On their way back into reality and away from the Disneyesque fairy-tale Christmas we had provided. It was snowing heavily. And this morning, the only morning it really snowed, we had to dig out as two of our brood had to get to the station. And there was no negotiation. We just couldn't say, 'stay until tomorrow and we'll see what the weather's like,' as they had a flight to catch.

So, we dug a tunnel out of our drive while the kids threw things in cases, updated Instagram pages and caught up with the last of *Cash in the Attic* on TV. Leaving three of them back at the ranch, we attempted the perilous ten-mile journey into town—made even more hazardous by the fact that the council in its wisdom hadn't gritted a single road. We slipped and slid all the way there and back, to be faced in the kitchen with every single pot and pan from cooking a full English, piled in the sink, and a magnificent snowman on the drive. Our adult children had used the time profitably to build us this amazing creation and decorated him with my husband's scarf (they were lucky there— all his scarves usually get left on trains), and a carrot nose of Pinocchio proportions. As we arrived home they were hunting for coal for eyes, and I just managed to stop them lifting the fake coal off our electric fire. I placated them instead with two pieces of Rocky Road which we had made for Christmas and could have used to repoint the brickwork.

And just then, I felt selfish. I wanted to say, 'Great snowman— what about the washing-up? Can we get the snowman to do it?' I felt irritated, resentful, fed-up and tired. I wasn't brimming with Christian charity and forbearance. I wanted a little help.

But five minutes later, I began to enjoy the snowman. He really was magnificent. And I began to think about it in another way. Our kids did what they wanted. Some may say they should have done the washing-up, but they took an hour out of their busy adult lives and enjoyed being kids again. They listened to their own needs and decided to play.

I'm thinking that maybe we could all do with a bit more of that. Yes, the washing-up still needs to be done—but we've decided that instead of angling for a spot in the Oxford Dictionary of Saints, we need to get the kids to help a little more, and then play a little more ourselves too. Be a bit selfish. Have some time for us.

Because ultimately, it is by looking after ourselves that we are better able to look after other people. When Jesus was really struggling with loads of people wanting him to heal them, he went off up a mountain by himself to pray. And I'm sure the disciples were saying, 'Where's he gone? He hasn't even cleared up breakfast! There's bits of fish around and everything ...'

It's back to balance—being whole people—as whole as we can be this side of eternity. And sometimes that means taking time for ourselves, whether it's building a snowman, going on a quiet day, or disappearing into the next room for five minutes' peace. It's about listening to what we need to in order to be most fulfilled and happy. Being aware of ourselves. And by doing that we become more able to listen to others and to God. Try it. It doesn't have to be complicated. Five minutes quiet. Half an hour with a book. Ten minutes knitting. Enjoy it. Say at the beginning of each day, 'What do I need for myself today? What will bring me to life?' 'How can I look after myself?' And then thank God for it.

Just do a rota for the washing-up this Christmas!

Eirene Palmer is Diocesan Spiritual Adviser for the Diocese of Derby. Her passions are family, writing and singing. She is published by BRF and Woman Alive *and co-leads ACW Café Writers in Derby alongside her husband Richard.*

Redeeming Grace

Emily Owen

We faced the double doors which led to theatre.
Only I could go through those doors.
When I came out, after surgery, I'd be deaf.
My parents knew the words they spoke now would be the
    last I'd ever hear.
'I love you.'
Three little words which say so much.
Three little words which followed me into theatre.
'I love you.'
It may even have been the first time my Dad had said them
    to me.
But he'd shown me my entire life.
I knew Dad loved me.

Ever since creation, even through creation, God has been
    saying,
I love you.
Sometimes people recognised that, but often they didn't.
God is still saying *I love you.*
Maybe you recognise that, maybe you don't.
Eventually God said,
I want you to know.
I long for you to know
my love.
So, I'm going to show you.
And Jesus came.
Which is what Christmas is all about.
The very best God could give you.

One Christmas, I taught a young choir to sing the carol
'Silent Night' in sign language.
I was only able to do so because, before I lost my hearing,
my mum insisted I learn to sign. I didn't want to. I
remember asking her why I'd want to learn sign
language.
I will never forget her answer:
'So we can communicate visually when you can't hear.'

Jesus,
coming as a baby at Christmas,
is God communicating visually when the world does not
hear.
Showing the world how much He loves us.
Showing you how much He loves you.

'Silent night! Holy night!
Son of God, Love's pure light;
Radiant beams from thy holy face,
With the dawn of redeeming grace,
Jesus, Lord, at thy birth.'

Maybe you think 'the dawn of redeeming grace' is for others,
not for you.
There's so much hurt, or anger, or fear, or bitterness, or
wrong in your life.
How can God's grace possibly reach that far?

The day my little goddaughter realised I am deaf, she said;
'It doesn't matter that you can't hear. You're still special.'

God says *it doesn't matter what you've done.*
It doesn't matter what you've not done.
You're still special.
Jesus came for you.

I gave the very best,
for you.

A 'dawn of redeeming grace'.
That's what Christmas is about.
A new beginning.
There is nothing God's grace cannot reach.
He loves you too much for that.

The night before I lost my hearing, I listened to Handel's
    Messiah.
On perhaps the most hopeless night in my life,
when I was about to become deaf forever,
I heard the words,
'For unto us a child is born …'

There is always hope.
And it starts with Jesus.

Who shall separate us from the love of Christ? Shall
tribulation, or distress, or persecution, or famine, or
nakedness, or danger, or sword? No, in all these things we
are more than conquerors through him who loved us. For I
am sure that neither death nor life, nor angels nor rulers, nor
things present nor things to come, nor powers, nor height
nor depth, nor anything else in all creation, will be able to
separate us from the love of God in Christ Jesus our Lord.

Romans 8: 35, 37–9

❄

Emily lost her hearing through surgery relating to a medical condition,
Neurofibromatosis Type 2. She is an inspirational speaker and author. Her
books include her 30 Days series, which aims to enthuse and engage people
with the Bible, and her memoir, Still Emily. *www.emily-owen.co.uk*

A Christmas Giftie

Fran Brady

SCOTLAND'S national poet, Robert Burns, wrote 'To a Louse' after observing the progress of one on a lady's hat in church.

Its most famous lines come in the last verse:

> O wad some pow'r the giftie gie us
> To see oursels as others see us!

I have often thought that such a 'giftie' would be a very mixed blessing. If you have ever caught sight of yourself unexpectedly in a mirror and thought 'who on earth is that old/untidy/ugly person?'—if you have ever torn up/deleted a photograph before anyone else sees it—you will know what I mean. Ignorance, if not actually bliss, then at least allows us to plod along through life in resigned acceptance of ourselves. But what if the giftie went further and allowed us to see ourselves as God sees us?

It was two days before Christmas, the 23rd December 2016. Like many loyal kirk-goers, I had signed up for the Church of Scotland's online Advent calendar—a daily email, consisting of a short video and a message. Each day had a one-word theme: peace; compassion; shelter; joy; etc. The part I enjoyed most came at the end: the background was always a Christmas tree, already sporting some decorations; a disembodied hand slipped into the picture with a tree bauble bearing the word for the day and hung it on a branch. It was effective and uplifting.

On the 23rd, sitting at breakfast with my iPad, I watched

the hand hang the bauble: the word for the day was 'faith'. Then my world rocked as I was flooded with intense emotion. The 23rd December is my oldest child's birthday: her name is Faith.

I suddenly experienced that incredible 'WOW! I DID THIS!' moment when your first baby is placed in your arms. I was filled with the same breathless joy, the same sense of instant lifelong commitment, the same love that makes all previous loves pale.

The feeling was so sudden, so unlooked-for, and so strong that I knew God was in it. As I gradually regained my balance and came back down to earth, I puzzled over the meaning of the experience. I decided that God was telling me that I should feel the same way about the babe in the manger as I had done about the babe in my arms many years ago. He was telling me that my love for and commitment to Jesus needed some work. Fair enough. I can put my hands up to that—who can't?

At least, that is what I thought God was saying to me. Just to be sure, I emailed a few of my Christian friends who are good at interpreting God's nudges. Within a couple of hours, I got back a very different interpretation. Remember Psalm 139, said my friends:

> For you formed my inward parts;
> you knitted me together in my mother's womb.
> I praise you for I am fearfully and wonderfully made.

God was telling me that *he* felt the same about *me* when he created me as I did about baby Faith when I birthed her all those years ago. And God is always the same: 'I am the Lord; I change not'. He is telling me that he still feels like that—every time he looks at me.

One of my other daughters (I have three) summed it up. When I told her the story, she shook her head and smiled.

'You always interpret God's signs and messages as reproof, spurs to improvement. Try to be open to a different kind of message—one of complete, delighted love. Remember that God 'rejoices over you with singing'.

How wonderful! What a Christmas gift!

Fran Brady lives near Edinburgh and her writing has a strong Scottish flavour. She has published four novels (www.franbrady.com) and is the chair of the Scottish Fellowship of Christian Writers (www.sfcw.info)

Christmas is for the Children

Lucy Rycroft

CHRISTMAS is for the children, isn't it? That's what they say, and they're right.

After all, children get loads of gifts—and they feel the pleasure of each one. The adults get socks and chocs, and say things like, 'I don't want anything this year' or 'Just give the money to charity instead'. You'll never catch a child refusing generosity like that.

And children spend hours carefully producing cards for those they love, adding an extra snowy-white pom-pom or shake of glitter, because there is no better way to spend an afternoon than creating something to give to someone precious. The adults cut corners and go for the quickest option, because there is just 'so much to do' and 'no time to stop'.

The films are just for kids too, aren't they? Crazy adventures and impossible fantasies where elves exist or animals talk. Grown-ups may indulge a made-up world for a couple of hours, but then they hit 'stop' on the remote control and get on with normal life.

Children stop and stare at Christmas lights for what seems like hours, awestruck by the sheer beauty of thousands upon thousands of tiny bulbs in all their myriad colours and shapes. Grown-ups, however, have the advantage—they've seen the lights before. They don't need to stare any harder or longer.

The Kingdom of heaven is for the children, isn't it? That's what He said (Mark 10:14), and He was right.

After all, children get loads of gifts—wisdom, knowledge, faith, healing, and more (1 Corinthians 12)—and they feel the pleasure of how each one helps to build the Body. The adults get what they've always got, and say things like, 'It's OK, you've given me enough already, God' and 'I don't need anything else, I'll just stick with what I've got', unaware that their modest stoicism might be depriving the church of something its Father wants to impart. You'll never catch a child refusing generosity like that.

And children spend hours reading, thinking, praying, listening in honour of the God they worship—because there is no better way to spend an afternoon than creating space to give to someone precious. The adults cut corners and scrimp on time with God, because there is just 'so much to do' and 'no time to stop'—while the children take pleasure in spending time with the God they love.

The weird, wonderful stories in the Bible are just for kids too, aren't they? Crazy adventures and impossible fantasies where the blind see and the dead are raised. Grown-ups may indulge this heavenly realm for a moment—but it's the children who continue to trust that God is still on top of His game in this area. They pray for the unexpected and the impossible, because they realise that miracles didn't stop with the death of the apostles.

Children stop and stare at the Light for what seems like hours, awestruck by the sheer beauty of thousands upon thousands of words, actions and feelings recorded for us. Grown-ups, however, have the advantage—they've seen the Light before. They don't need to stare any harder or longer at Him.

Children, however, know the secret. The secret that you can always look harder, look longer, and find facets of this Light that you never noticed were there before. This Light, after all, is the embodiment of the God who made the Universe. How could there not always be more to see?

Christmas is for the children—children who are defined not by age or maturity, but by trust and priorities.

Truly, I say to you, whoever does not receive the kingdom of God like a child shall not enter it. (Mark 10:15)

This Christmas let us all be like children to inherit the Kingdom of heaven—the Kingdom which is already here on earth, a little bit, but is also in the future, when our Heavenly Father once again sends His Son down to us, to complete the job.

Lucy Rycroft is just emerging from the haze of early parenthood. A former teacher, she now blogs about family life, parenting, adoption and faith at desertmum.wordpress.com, and writes regularly for the Home for Good website.

Another Christmas

Paul Trembling

ALL stories are about the past, for the past affects everything that happens now and all that will happen in the future. Every story is 'once upon a time'.

But not all stories have the same past. This story is one of long ago, but probably not the long ago you are familiar with.

In my story, there was a young woman, hardly more than a girl really, and one night she woke to a glorious vision. A being, human-like but not human, appeared before her. And it shone with a brilliant light, and it spoke with a voice of great beauty, and it said to her, 'You are the most blessed of women, for you will have a child, and he shall be the Messiah.'

(And now you are thinking that you know this story after all. But read on.)

And the young woman said, 'No! I do not want this child! I do not want this blessing!'

You can understand her reasoning. She was after all, a virgin and unmarried. In fact, she was engaged—but if she was found to be with child, the engagement would be broken off, she would be humiliated and probably cast out. No one was going to believe any story of glowing creatures.

But the angel (for so we can presume it was) said, 'It will be as it will be.' And then it vanished from her sight, and that part of the story was done, told, and in the past.

In due course, it happened as the angel had said, and the young woman—might as well call her Mary, it's what you're used to—became pregnant.

When her fiancé found out, he was furious and broke off the engagement immediately.

The angel appeared to him and told him he should take her

back and raise the child as his own, for this was of God. But that was a step of faith too far, and he said so.

So Mary was packed off to her distant cousin—an older woman who herself had unexpectedly become pregnant. They were a devout family, and not best pleased at having this young relative of questionable morals foisted upon them. But Mary's cousin found herself glad of the company, and her husband had been struck dumb by the shock of it all and so could not object with any success.

It was a time of political and economic turmoil but Mary, out in the sticks, avoided the worst of it. As her time came near, she reflected that if her marriage had gone ahead she would have been forced to go travelling with her husband in accordance with the latest tax laws, and in her condition that might have ended very badly.

As it was, she gave birth in the relative comfort of her cousin's home.

That night, there were shepherds out in the fields tending their flocks, who suddenly saw a great and terrifying vision of angels who told them to go into Bethlehem to meet the newborn Messiah. So, they went but of course the Messiah wasn't there and they returned to their flocks disappointed and short of a day's pay, docked for absenteeism.

Some years later, Wise Men from the East had similar problems. Their guiding star proved inaccurate, and they took their gifts back home with them. On the plus side, King Herod was reassured that he had no rivals to worry about, and the children of Jerusalem grew up with no more than the usual childhood problems.

And so the story continued in a very different way from the one we are familiar with. Of course, the child grew, and being the same child, found his own way to fulfil that Messiahship. There could still have been a baptism: perhaps, growing up with his cousin, he might have assisted in the baptising. In due course, perhaps there were disciples. Almost certainly there would have been miracles, and parables, and teaching, and angry Pharisees who would probably have raked up the scandal of his birth to discredit him.

There could still have been a death and a resurrection.

But with this version of the story, the winter solstice remains a pagan festival. We'd celebrate New Year, but there wouldn't have been much of a Christmas story to give cause for celebration. A straightforward and uneventful birth doesn't attract much attention outside the immediate family.

You see, all stories are about the past. But if there was no past, or no past of note, then there would be no story worth telling. We have the story we have because a Master Story Teller ensured that the events we now call Christmas happened as they should have.

Our present relies on the past which he wove into the story.

Paul Trembling is 60 but acts older. He currently lives in Bath and spends as much time as possible writing!

Mince Pies

Richard Palmer

D ID you know that the eating of mince pies at Christmas is still illegal in this country? Apparently, Oliver Cromwell banned Christmas puddings, mince pies and anything to do with the celebration of Christmas. He thought eating such things was a lewd act. Oliver was probably one of the world's greatest party poopers and not the sort you'd have round for a congenial supper or a couple of drinks of a Saturday night to watch the football. And as for his wife Elizabeth, I don't expect she got out much or had the opportunity to enjoy some of the fripperies of life, such as popping down the stylists to get her highlights done.

But the amazing fact is that the law has never been rescinded, so that mince pies, like Class A drugs, are illegal. Beware, if there's a knock on your door on Christmas Day and you see a blue-uniformed figure through the window, or someone resembling a Roundhead. My advice is to flush the pies or give them to the dog, or you might be in trouble with the law. And be careful driving during Advent in case you get breathalysed for mincemeat in your bloodstream.

It's a crazy notion, illegal mince pies, and I'm trying to imagine a world in which this were true. There would be a mince-pie underworld run by local barons. There would be mince-pie speakeasies down dark alleys, offering genuine home-cooked pies, served with lashings of clotted cream or brandy butter. There'd be dodgy dealers on street corners, sidling up and offering you genuine 100% homemade mincemeat for home consumption. And those nice waggy-tailed spaniels at Heathrow would be retrained to pick out the divine scent of sweet spices, preserved fruit and pastry.

When something is banned, we become more interested in it.

When it's freely available, we lose such interest. It's one of the freedoms in our democratic society that we are free to believe in and practice our Christian faith or to believe in any other for that matter. Perhaps we take that too much for granted. There are countries where people do not have that freedom. You do not need to read too far into any daily newspaper to find stories of the persecution and repression of Christian faith.

At Christmas, we are all free to go to church. I wonder what would happen if the government told us we couldn't. There would be an outcry and we'd all campaign for the right and we'd try to exercise it. Or alternatively, what if we were told we had to? We'd rebel again.

In fact, when Cromwell banned the celebration of Christmas, this caused the Plum Pudding Riots (no, it's not a Ken Dodd fantasy!) and soldiers were called to several cities to quell the protests against the banning of Christmas celebrations.

You see, our human nature is that we like the freedom to choose. And that's what God gave us, our free will, the right to choose whether we believe in him or not. And likewise, we all have the choice of how we celebrate Christmas, whether as the celebration of Christ's birth or an excuse for an overindulgent family holiday. We are free to choose.

But before you go rushing off to conceal your Sainsbury's Taste the Difference mince pies in the attic, I have a confession to make to you—that this piece of information about illegal mince pies is in fact an urban myth, or to dress it in more modern clothes, it's fake news. In fact, it's so fake that the BBC reporting in an article in April 2012 on 'legal legends' specifically mentioned this myth of illegal mince pies. The ban did not survive when Charles II became king. So, you can relax this Christmas and tuck in with a clear conscience. Those Plum Pudding Riots, which actually did occur, clearly had a lasting impact.

So, here are two free choices you have this Christmas: you can legitimately eat mince pies and you can legitimately go to church. And this is the paradox. We are all free to go to church on Christmas Day, compared with those parts of the world where it is either not possible or extremely dangerous to do so or compared to those times such as Cromwell's when it was banned. But too few do come to our churches.

It's a time of year when we do get new faces through the doors, often those who want to do something spiritually to mark Christmas but don't know quite how to meet that vague desire that they sense throughout the rest of the year as well. And we all have to ask ourselves a very deep and meaningful question this Christmas. What do we need to do to truly encourage these seekers to come back? It's the church's biggest challenge and one that every church must apply its collective mind to. Because if we don't, we won't see them again until next year. Or maybe never again at all.

And the odds are that we will do Christmas the same this year in our churches as every other year and carry on with the same protocols, practices and services throughout the year and then wonder why no new faces are appearing. As someone once said, 'The definition of insanity is doing the same thing over and over again, expecting different results.' It is one worth pinning up on your church notice board.

And if all else fails in your creative thinking on Christmas services, at least you now know that you can relax and offer, with impunity, free mince pies …

Richard Palmer is a writer, coach and spiritual accompanier and facilitates days exploring the spiritual journey, discernment and vocations. He is secretary to the Derby Diocese Spirituality Group and with his wife, Eirene, co-leads Café Writers, the Derby Christian Writers group.

Jesus the Word

Sheila Johnson

In the beginning was the Word, and the Word was with God, and the Word was God. He was in the beginning with God. All things were made through him, and without him was not anything made that was made. In him was life, and the life was the light of men. The light shines in the darkness, and the darkness has not overcome it.

THE first five verses of John's Gospel are deeply significant to me as a writer and as a Christian. These verses, often read at Christmas time, have always filled me with awe and reverence.

We are all creative in some way or other whether we write, craft, cook, paint or, in fact, anything we put our skills towards, and God's anointing can be seen in the finished product, even if unacknowledged. The fact that Jesus was the very first Word ever uttered makes everything we do significant. Our gifts reflect the nature and character of our Creator, the ultimate creator. Verse 3 says that all things came into being by Him and apart from him nothing could come into being. This is creativity of the highest order. His creation is born and without His breath being breathed into plant, animal or human being, his word spoken over them, they can't exist. He is the Word to end all words. The Alpha and Omega of Words.

In verse 5 it says that God is light and His Word shines into all the dark places, places filled with evil and a darkness so great and overwhelming that it cannot hope to understand the light of God's revelation, his created glory. As well as being creative, we are all hardwired to do bad and evil things, but how encouraging that God's light can shine into the dark corners of each of our lives, exposing all our dark thoughts and feelings and in exchange filling them with his light, his glory and his Word. We are filled with the Word, with Jesus. It is also encouraging to know that however dark that darkness can sometimes feel or become in our lives it can never hope to block out God's love, light or presence, which is always stronger.

As Christians, our giftings can be redemptive, as we restore our world through the power of our creativity. We can only hope and pray that some of our created gifts help to reflect just a little of the Creator's glory and light and help to expose the darkness around us, as we fulfil his purposes for our creativity and our lives.

In the beginning was the word,
the word to end all words, to write all unfinished stories.
His word is my word and that word is life,
the ultimate meaning to kick-start a world,
breathe breath into being.

His word was also the final agony of dying,
last breath, riven with hope to raise the dead
and once again fill the world with light.

Sheila Johnson, a qualified journalist and article writer, produced her first book, Alpha Male, *a romance based round an Alpha Course, a couple of years ago.* Waireka, *a historical romance set in nineteenth century New Zealand was published in June 2018.*

Tinsel and Turkey

All the Trimmings of Christmas

While Shoppers Thronged

Sue Richards

While shoppers thronged the streets tonight
And snapped up Christmas cheer,
A baby boy was quietly born
In a stable dark and drear.

'I'm here,' he called to passers-by
And some went in and stared,
But others kept on buying gifts;
They hadn't really cared.

As they rushed home to write the cards
And decorate the tree,
They didn't see him waiting, or
His wish to set them free.

The lights are up, the cake's been baked
It's party time again.
They're much too busy having fun
To think about his pain.

'We're having goose for lunch this year,
Of course, it costs much more,
But we're not having Auntie Flo,
She really is a bore.'

The cards show Santa filling sacks
Or robins in the snow.
But who's the cute babe in the crib?
Nobody seems to know.

He is the King, the Lord of Life
Who came because we sin.
God's gift to us at Christmas time
If we'd just let him in.

So, celebrate with all your heart
And hands and mind and voice.
Enjoy the riches of his grace,
And in his love rejoice.

Sue Richards lives in Newport Pagnell, where she is a member of the Baptist church and teaches Functional Skills English to adults, as well as caring for members of her family. She leads MK Torch Fellowship for visually impaired people and has written ever since she could hold a pen.

The Boy who Wanted Everything

Anna Adeney

IT'S Advent, *at last!*' James jumped up and down. 'Can I write my Christmas list now?'

He adored everything about Christmas—the food, shop displays, decorations. Christmas carols and even church services, especially Christingle, were also on his other list. The one saying things to love about Christmas. These things gave him a nice, warm, Christmassy glow. But what James loved most was presents. His toy catalogues were practically worn away by December. He wanted *everything!*

His parents sighed. They loved Christmas too, but for different reasons.

James began:

> mobile phone (I AM old enuff!)
> books +++
> rollerblades
> magnetic construction kit
> radio-controlled car
> chocolate +++++
> luminous watch
> torch
> video games …

He printed out the long list on the computer. He gave all his relatives a copy and mailed one to Santa. All December, James went on wanting and wanting and *wanting*. On Christmas Eve his family hung up their stockings on the mantelpiece. He put a mince pie, decorated with a sprig of holly, on a red plate for Santa.

James was so excited, thinking about all his presents. When he heard his parents go to bed, he grabbed his sleeping bag, crept downstairs and hid behind the sofa. He wanted to see Santa for himself! A few hours later a sound woke him up. He peered over the back of the sofa. Santa was there, but something was wrong! James knew that Santa was a jolly, happy soul. But Santa looked miserable!

'Come out, James,' came a gruff voice. 'I know you're there.'

Confused, James did as he was told. 'Why are you so sad?' he asked.

'I'm sad about children,' said Santa, 'Like *you*, James!'

'But why?' asked James, very puzzled. 'Christmas is a happy time!'

'You love the presents I bring,' said Santa, 'But you've missed the *true* meaning of Christmas. That makes me very sad!'

'I don't understand!'

'You can see, hear, touch, smell and taste Christmas,' said Santa. 'But those are just the symbols. Do you know what a symbol is?'

'It's something that stands for something else,' said James. 'Like, two golden arches mean MacDonald's.'

'Correct!' said Santa. 'Can I tell you what Christmas symbols *really* mean?'

'Yes, please.'

'Look at that green Christmas tree,' said Santa. 'Green is the symbol of the hope of eternal life that Jesus brings. The tree needles point upwards, towards heaven. That's where our thoughts should always be directed.'

'I never knew that!' said James.

'See the bright star on the top?' said Santa. 'Remember how the star led the wise men to the stable in Bethlehem? It's the symbol of promise. God promised us a Saviour and the star pointed the way to where God fulfilled that promise with the birth of Jesus. It shows that God *always* keeps his promises and that men should still seek him.'

'I never knew that!' said James.

Santa pointed at the red ornaments. 'The second Christmas colour is red,' he said. 'Red is the colour of our life-giving blood. God gave his son, Jesus, so that the shedding of his blood would give us eternal life. Red reminds us of God's greatest gift, which is better than *any* presents that anyone could ever give you!'

'I never knew that!' said James.

Santa pointed to the twinkling lights. 'Light is a symbol of us showing our thanks to God for his precious gift. He wants *us* to do good in the world. We can shine like lights for him. Remember when that new boy came to school? Everyone was mean to him because he had a funny accent and thick glasses? But *you* asked him to play with you and soon everyone played with him too. You were a shining light for Jesus that day, James.'

'I never knew that!' said James.

Santa took a candy-cane and held it upside down. 'Candy-cane is a hard white sweet, striped with red. The white reminds us that Jesus was sinless and pure. The red stripes remind us that the soldiers whipped him. It also looks like a shepherd's crook, ready to rescue sheep from danger. It reminds us that God is the Good Shepherd and always ready to rescue *us* when we get lost, just like sheep. It's also shaped like a letter J for Jesus.'

'I never knew that!' said James.

Santa selected the mince pie. 'These are Christmas symbols too. Years ago, Christians believed that Christ's crown of thorns was made of holly. The berries were white but turned red from the blood flowing from his head. Today's mince pies are round and sweet, but originally, they were made of minced meat. The meat was baked in oblong pastry cases to symbolise Christ's crib and three spices were always added to represent the gifts given to Jesus by the three Wise Men.'

'I never knew that!' said James.

Santa picked up a wreath. 'This wreath contains *all* the good things about Christmas for those with eyes to see and hearts to understand. It is green and red, with the heaven-turned needles of the evergreen. The bow reminds us of what ties *us* all together——that perfect bond that is love. It's a circle, without beginning and without end. That's the eternity of God's love, which goes on forever.'

'I never knew that!' said James.

'These are the symbols I want you to understand—and tell your friends about,' said Santa.

'But what about *you*, Santa?' asked James.

Santa laughed, jolly and happy again. 'I'm the spirit of family fun, and I *do* symbolise presents. The wise men brought the first gifts for the baby Jesus and now we give presents every year on his birthday. But we must never forget that God gave us the best gift of all—his son Jesus.'

'I knew *that*!' said James. 'Perhaps thinking about presents so much made me forget. But now you've told me about all those symbols, I'll *never* forget.'

And he never did. The boy who wanted everything had learnt the true meaning of Christmas.

Anna Adeney has had nearly 50 children's books published (as Anne Adeney), as well as many works in story, poetry and educational anthologies. She also has an MA in Creative Writing. She is just returning to the writing scene after ten years of serious illness and finds herself woefully behind the times of modern children's fiction!

3 D Jesus

April McIntyre

DECORATING the house just before Christmas is one of the jobs I particularly enjoy, however busy I may be. There's a special thrill in unpacking boxes of ornaments that have been acquired over the years and finding just the right place for them downstairs, together with branches of holly and rosemary out of the garden, some geriatric strands of coloured tinsel to bedeck the picture frames and plenty of candles to create a festive look. Over the top? Surely not. It's strange how simple objects can acquire such rich associations: old friends to be treated with respect and a smile.

Like my Advent stable. Originally, it was a cardboard model of the Nativity which you assembled piece by piece throughout December, constructing the simple building with its cattle stall and animals, odd bits of vegetation, star, angel, familiar shepherds and wise men. Finally, on Christmas morning, a tiny cardboard baby would be slotted into the cardboard manger to complete the story. Naturally, it wasn't very robust. A door opening suddenly or a vicious jolt from the vacuum cleaner and half the stable characters would be flattened, swept together into unspiritual heaps. Nevertheless, there was a certain charm in moving the figures around in that timeless drama, especially in the evenings when all became a little magical in the flickering candlelight.

It reminded me of the story of St. Francis of Assisi and how he created the very first nativity scene back in the 13th century in the small town of Greccio in central Italy. Francis wanted to invite all the local people to celebrate the birth of Jesus, but the village church wasn't big enough. Instead, he set up a wooden manger in a cave on the hillside with real animals and a couple of locals as Mary and Joseph. The ordinary folk flocked up the hill with their torches: the baker and blacksmith, mothers, children, soldiers, beggars, farmers, shopkeepers. As his monks sang, Francis told how God chose to come as a tiny baby to ordinary people just like them, born in a poor stable in Bethlehem.

Today we still use this simple way into the Christmas story, whether we're infants in tea towels and dressing gowns or world-weary adults. It's not so important to know the exact time of year when it all happened, the true number of wise men or whether Jesus was born in a stable, a cave or a house. We just want to feel that, somehow, we can slip in at the back, coming with all our doubts, questions, and yearnings, and be welcome.

Consequently, last Christmas there I was again, happily assembling my Advent stable, surrounded by white and silver tree decorations and half-unpacked boxes. So, imagine my horror when I discovered that baby Jesus was gone. All the other figures were there, the stable structures were intact, but no amount of searching the carpet on hands and knees produced any revelation. Would my little cardboard crib have to remain empty?

I considered creating a replacement cardboard baby, but, in the end, decided my drawing skills weren't quite up to it. So, after some deliberation, I improvised with a pinch of modelling clay and some towelling to create a tiny 3D Jesus. His round face and pin-prick eyes looked up at me, swathed in towelling strips. I placed him (a little premature) on the cardboard manger.

Suddenly, I realised a cataclysmic event had taken place in the cardboard cut-out stable. 3D Jesus introduced a whole new dimension into the flat and flimsy world of Cardboard Nativity. A greater reality. Something 'more'.

No longer was it enough just to look at the stable and tweak the figures from time to time. 3D Jesus was inviting me to touch, feel, interact; welcoming God incarnate through this tiny, passive bundle of clay and rags. He was something to hold, to carry around in a pocket, to pray with. He warmed my heart in a rather disturbing way, this clay Immanuel. Somehow he needed me to tell his story and help him live.

I thought again of the story of St Francis and what I had always considered the rather fanciful conclusion to that nativity tale where one of Francis' followers, gazing at the manger, cries out that he sees a beautiful baby lying there. Was it really Jesus? A miracle, a vision? Whatever it was, the people of Greccio were sure that God's son had been with them in a very special way and continued to praise God through the night. God has a knack of getting close to us, sometimes in surprising ways.

I wonder what kind of Jesus will be found in your home over Christmas. Will he be a flimsy, Hollywood stereotype or something with a little more substance: a 3D Jesus? Perhaps he'll be a trusted saviour and friend, filling life with purpose and joy. One thing I know for sure, having encountered 3D Jesus you really can't go back to a cardboard cut-out.

> Come, Lord Jesus,
> come into our everyday reality.
> Help us not to be content
> with what is flat and flimsy
> but lead us into new dimensions
> of life and adventure,
> not just for Christmas
> but for all eternity.
>
> Amen.

April McIntyre is a licensed lay minister at St. Michael's, Breaston in Derbyshire and uses creative ways of communicating as an integral part of her work. A member of Derby Café Writers Group, April enjoys writing reflections, prayers and poems and is a reviewer for The Reader *magazine.*

Two Sonnets in Search of Christmas

Geoff Daniel

I

'I can't find Christmas!' Just a week before
The Day, my wife in organising mode
hit a blank: somewhere we'd stashed it, a load
of lights and baubles, tinfoil star and more,

packed away a year ago. The tree was bare,
and all the lovely ornament-bright things
our children crafted once, angels with wings,
the salt-dough beasts, all their work—was nowhere.

(…Until an old, unlikely cedar chest
in desperation was checked—and there they were,
each special piece, held in the scented air
for the Nordman fir waiting to be dressed.)

Believer, do not scorn this joy as shallowness:
love has its histories, the greater and the less.

II

'You shouldn't have!' The presents pile in stacks
under the tree of brilliance, each bound
in colour and design, some tied around
with gold, some bowed, some tagged; and if one lacks
the finesse of another's wrapping, we indulge—
it's the thought that counts; it's the care that lends

the gesture life, and makes the choice that sends
the message right.
What is this shape? This bulge?
What clever and predictive games we've played
to find the perfect gift that will surprise,
that'll strike a chord and delight the eyes
when the paper's off, and the thing's displayed.

Ah, Christian, do not scorn this getting and giving:
it was taught us by the love that keeps us living.

An English teacher for 38 years, Geoff Daniel has published numerous poems and one collection, besides articles and Bible study notes. The ACW Poetry Adviser, he writes critiques of members' poems, and has run workshops and competitions.

The Christmas Onion

Graeme Smith

IF there was an award for the vegetable most associated with Christmas, I think it would be won by the Brussels sprout, with parsnips and carrots as runners up. It certainly wouldn't be won by the onion, although the onion would probably be a strong contender for 'best supporting vegetable' for its role in the stuffing and the gravy. However, I think that the onion is in fact very closely connected to Christmas, because like onions (and, if you have seen the film Shrek, like ogres) Christmas has many layers.

The first layer is the personal 'traditions' which we establish in our families and other relationships. My family 'traditions' include unpacking socks full of random trinkets (always including a toothbrush!) first thing on Christmas morning, eating Christmas dinner a few days before Christmas, rather than on Christmas Day, and hanging a saxophone-playing gnome on our Christmas tree (don't ask!). It is because of these 'traditions' that my son says that his in-laws 'don't do Christmas properly'. No doubt they say the same about us!

Going deeper, the next layer is the traditions built up over time by the culture in which we live. For me, this includes Christmas trees and decorations, turkey with all the trimmings and mince pies, Father Christmas and gift-wrapped presents. In a different culture, we will experience a mix of the familiar, the unfamiliar, and the downright weird. Over time, these traditions can change, so we complain that Christmas 'isn't like it used to be when I was a child'.

The next layer looks religious. But it is deceptive. It is the Christmas of cards, nativity plays, and even carols. The virgin Mary has a halo and is unfeasibly serene and unruffled as a new

226

mother. There are three kings with camels. Three ships come sailing in on Christmas Day in the morning. Animals bow down to worship the baby as 'no crying he makes.' Snow has fallen, 'snow on snow; snow on snow'. And there is a donkey—always a donkey. But none of these things is biblical—not even the donkey (check it out: donkeys only appear in the gospels on Palm Sunday and in the parable of the good Samaritan). This is a safe and comfortable Christmas.

We're nearly there as we get to the next layer—the brutal reality of the first Christmas. The teenage virgin discovering that she is pregnant, living in a society where extra-marital sex would lead to stoning. The shock and doubts of her fiancé as he discovers this. The exhausting journey ending in giving birth in a strange location. Ritually unclean shepherds visiting the baby. Gentile philosophers travelling in search of a child. A power-hungry king ruthlessly ordering the murder of children. Another journey, this time as refugees to a foreign land, fleeing danger. Blood, sweat, toil and tears.

And finally we reach the heart of Christmas. A baby—Emmanuel, God with us. God with us in the shocks, the doubts and the fears. God with us in the familiar, the unfamiliar and the downright weird. God with us in our families and relationships. God with us in the religious and the traditions. God with us in our searching. God with us in times of trouble. God with us in times of change. God with us in the safe and the comfortable. God with us in our blood, sweat, toil and tears. And God with us on the journey, wherever and whenever we are going.

So this Christmas, how deep will you go? Will you be content with traditions and a safe, comfortable Christmas? Or, as the onion gravy infuses the whole of your dinner, will you let God infuse the whole of your life?

Graeme Smith is a Circuit Judge; a husband, father and grandfather; an elder and preacher in his local church; and an occasional author. He combined law and faith to write Was the tomb empty? A lawyer weighs the evidence for the resurrection *(published by Monarch).*

Wrapsody

Linda Hunter

Christmas glints in vintage baubles
Childhood memories, snow dusted.
Strung with (gummed) paper chains
Callow, untarnished.
The unvarnished years

Before
Frosting was sweet taboo,
Family feasts were off the menu,
The annual bonanza gave way
To yet sweeter climes
Where tallow took centre stage: Christingle times.

Then that strange interlude
When no light shone
And even the matches were damp.

Christmas present comes ready wrapped:
A divine space, diffused with grace
Where we await,
Celebrate
The re-birth of love.

Linda Hunter is working her way around our great cathedrals (with the occasional foray abroad) while indulging her twin passions of art and nature.
   Her writing meanders equally: from poetry to magazine articles, devotionals to outlines for Scripture Union and recipes to children's stories.

Excuse Me?

Robin Carmichael

'WHAT,' warbled a robin, 'has Christmas to do with me?'

'Maybe,' mumbled the gatepost on which the robin was standing, 'Christmas isn't to do with you; it has to do with me, though I'm blowed if I know what or how or why.'

'Perhaps,' whispered a snowy village scene, 'it is actually about me. I mean, although I say it myself, I do look—well—rather nice. But what have I to do with Christmas?'

'Suppose,' chuckled a plump man with a red coat, white beard, black belt and cheery smile as he steered a flying sledge laden with parcels and hauled by several gravity-defying reindeer. 'Suppose it is to do with me. Everyone likes a plump man with a red coat, white beard, black belt and a cheery smile who doles out presents that no one actually has to pay for.' He said the last few words with his fingers crossed behind his back because he knew it wasn't true. 'And,' he added, 'they call me Father Christmas, but I've quite forgotten why.'

'Gulp,' gobbled the turkey, 'glig bubbly gurgle nobly kakawooblik aratikly ermapendump. Christmas.'

'Quite,' observed one of the reindeer.

'What about me?' blurted the fairy on top of a plastic tree on a table next to a log fire. 'Everyone tells me I'm a great tradition atop a Christmas tree, but nobody has told me what the tradition is or what this Christmas thing is.'

'Talking of trees,' murmured a five-foot-tall spruce tree wedged into a large plant pot in the corner of a sitting room. 'I wish they'd let me grow to the height I'm supposed to be. Furthermore, they festoon me with lights, tinsel, baubles and other such frippery. I'm a serious tree. God knows why they call me a Christmas tree.'

'Did someone mention my name?' asked a kindly voice that seemed to come from nowhere in particular.

The robin, the gatepost, the snowy village scene, the plump man with a red coat, the turkey, the fairy and the spruce tree all fell silent. Then, quite by chance, they all said together: 'Excuse me?'

'Somebody,' said the kindly voice, 'mentioned God. And you all mentioned Christmas. Is there a problem?'

All the things in this story began to talk at once. The noise was unspeakable, but they gradually drifted into an embarrassed silence.

The snowy village scene cleared its throat. 'Actually, we don't remember what Christmas is.'

'Ah,' said the kindly voice. Twice. 'OK. Fine. The thing is, all of you make people feel happier, so that is good when you think about it. Agreed?'

They all nodded which showed they agreed.

'Is that all?' perked up the gatepost.

'No, it is not all,' said the kindly voice. 'But it is a good start, don't you think?'

They all nodded.

'The difficulty,' resumed the kindly voice, 'is that the real, bigger, better, most amazing and wonderful reason for feeling happier is quite hard to understand. Can any of you draw?'

They all shook their heads.

'Well, I'm not good at drawing either,' said the kindly voice 'but I'm very good at creating things—like every single thing you can think of.'

'Wow,' chorused the chorus of Christmassy things that make people happier.

'Yes,' continued the kindly voice. 'So, Mary, the world's greatest lady, gave birth to a baby called Jesus. And when he grew up he was Love in a human form. Christmas is his birthday.'

There was a long hush, then the kindly voice said, 'Lots of people believe this, but lots of people don't.'

The voice dropped to a whisper. 'Christmas is *my* birthday.'

There was a longer hush and then a tiny, gentle whisper. 'I am God. God is Love. I lived as a human.'

Silence gripped the universe. Then all creation asked, 'Why?'

'Because,' the whisper was barely audible, 'I love you. Christ means Saviour and "-mas" is the ceremony of people meeting to say, "thank you". Christ-mas.'

Silence again. Some plops like tears falling on a lake echoed round the universe. Then an even softer, gentler whisper could just be heard: 'They have almost forgotten. Tell them. Tell them that I love them.'

Robin Carmichael has worked as a waiter, a Parachute Regiment Officer, a medical missionary, a GP, a Hospice physician and an author. Now well into the joys of retirement he still writes, enjoys his wonderful family and star-gazing with an equally wonderful telescope.

A for the Angels:
a Christmas Alphabet

Lance Pierson

A for the Angels who sang to God's glory
B for the Baby, the point of the story
C for the Carols we sing and we play
D for December, the 25th day
E is for Everyone, friendly and nice!
F for the Frost and the snow and the ice
G is for Greetings the post-person brings
H is for Hanging them up on long strings
I is for 'I wish that Christmas would come!'
J is for Jesus—he invented the fun
K—the three Kings, who travelled so far
L for the Light of the beckoning star
M is for Mistletoe—a kiss and a blush
N—now it's Night-time, to bed in a rush
O is for Open eyes, late Christmas Eve
P for the Presents we hope we'll receive
Q is for 'Quiet', Mum tells us to keep
R is for Restless—we can't go to sleep
S for the Stockings found bulging to burst
T for the Tree—Who can open up first?
U is Unwrapping, and cheering each winner
V is the Vast, extra-specially big dinner
W—Worth all the Wanting and Waiting
X is for Xmas—top of the ratings
Y is for You'n'me—all these things please us
Z—ZZZZZ at the end: thank you, great Jesus.

Lance Pierson is an actor, specialising in performing poetry, the Bible and one-man shows. He seldom has time to write now, but in a previous century he wrote fifteen books and was Vice-Chairman of the Association of Christian Writers.

Traditions Die Hard

Jennifer Allong-Bratt

'MUM, can I open my presents, please?' I implored to my mother's retreating back as she bustled into the kitchen. Completely ignoring me she busied herself preparing the turkey and ham for the oven while the freshly kneaded dough was set to rise on another corner of the kitchen counter. Nobody can make freshly baked bread as my mother did, to this very day.

It was a tradition in our household that my sisters and I always got new nightgowns for Christmas amongst other gifts. They were always so lovely. My nine-year-old excited self couldn't wait for Christmas morning to open presents, especially to find my long-awaited new nightgown! I wanted to go to sleep wearing it and to wake up on Christmas morning feeling warm and cuddly and … yes, beautiful!

Then a voice from the kitchen. 'We are going to midnight mass and it is almost 11 o'clock and you haven't started getting ready as yet!'

'Please, Mum, there's still enough time to open presents, it's only 9 o'clock. I have two whole hours to get ready.'

'Tell your sisters to get ready for Mass and you too, and when you get back home you can open a present, but only one,' my mother warned.

I was ecstatic! The promise that I could open at least one present propelled me to the bedroom. I couldn't get ready fast enough even though it was a short walk to the neighbourhood Catholic Church. In those days, almost everyone in our community went to midnight mass and we would meet and greet neighbours and friends on the way. I miss those days.

Needless to say, I couldn't concentrate on the Mass. My behaviour was almost robot-like throughout the service. All I could think of was what my new nightgown would look like. What colour would it be? Would it be long or would it be short? Would it be embroidered or plain? How would it feel against my skin? All these questions rambling through my head when suddenly, I felt a nudge from one of my sisters. It was communion time. Even though I am much older than nine now, these considerations when buying a new nightgown or pair of pyjamas still affect my choices to this day.

I couldn't wait for Mass to be over. I took our stairs by leaps and bounds. In spite of the wonderful aroma of baking turkey and ham emanating out of the kitchen and assailing my nostrils, the smells of which were irresistible, I delved under the Christmas tree. I proceeded to squeeze every package with my name on it, trying to find the one I thought held my nightgown. After much digging and squeezing, finally holding a package aloft, I triumphantly shouted, 'Ah! I've found it!' and immediately started ripping apart the beautiful wrapping to reveal a white cotton nightgown. It was embroidered in vivid bright colours to the front, long, which I had hoped for, and I somehow knew it would reach to my ankles. I couldn't wait to put it on and awake Christmas morning feeling, well, almost beautiful. A different person from the one who went to bed the night before. Much like hearing the Christmas message preached year on year, having the effect of transforming us into beautiful and different people for the glory of God.

Christmas has always been my favourite time of the year. In spite of all the commercialism which we didn't experience as children, I still remember the sights, smells and sounds of all those past Christmases at home with my parents. Dad and my brother doing all the manly preparations, we girls helping Mum with the last-minute hanging of new curtains and the baking of the traditional fruit cake. I'm excited when Christmas comes around and I still uphold the traditions that I grew up with. The joys of wrapping presents and decorating my home. Cooking, baking and entertaining guests. Going to church service, except not always at midnight. And yes, I still awake on Christmas morning in new nightwear, having the same feelings as I did when I was nine years old. But now the most important part is hearing the gospel preached and understanding all over again the real reason for Christmas and that Jesus is the ultimate Gift—as wonderful a tradition as the gift of a new nightgown.

Mum is now in her nineties and when Christmas rolls around, I can sense her longing for the good old days. She wants all her children around her and all the traditions of a bygone Christmas. When she calls me from abroad, I hear a wistfulness in her voice when she asks, 'Are you coming home for Christmas? If you are, all I want is a small ham, that's all.' Smiling to myself I respond, 'I don't think I can make it this Christmas, but we'll see,' anticipating the delight on her face when I unexpectedly turn up and knowing full well that I had already booked my flight and packed my suitcase. Among the things I am taking for her is— you guessed it! A brand-new nightgown!

Jennifer Allong-Bratt is a trained Christian Counsellor and budding writer. She lives part-time in London and in the US and gets most of her inspiration whilst travelling. She has taken up photography and intends that travel writing will become her new career in the not too distant future. She is delighted as this is her first published piece of work.

The Medley Carol
(a confusion of good news)

Jan Godfrey

1

On Christmas night all Christians sing
'How still we see thee lie'—
While shepherds watched their flocks by night
Three ships came sailing by!

2

In Royal David's city once
Those frosty winds made moan;
And good King Wenceslas looked out—
But the holly bears the crown.

3

God rest you merry, gentlemen!
Who offer gifts most rare—
How far is it to Bethlehem?
Oh ... *OH* ... ... that we were there ...

4

But hark! The herald angels sing,
As *SHARP!!* as any thorn;
It came upon the midnight clear
That Jesus Christ was born.

5

Good Christian men, rejoice and sing
Ere Adam lay y-bound;

The cattle? They are lowing,
All seated on the ground ...

6
... then, from the realms of glory—
A partridge in a tree!
Nowell, Nowell, Nowell, Nowell!—
Rejoice and merry be!

Tune: FOREST GREEN
(*Oh Little Town of Bethlehem*)

❈

Jan Godfrey has belonged to ACW for many years and won awards for poetry. Her published children's books include The Cherry Blossom Tree, Oliver and The Big Green Snake, *and* Yellow Wellies.

Light in the Darkness

Christmas when Times are Tough

Just Enough Light in the Darkness

Dave Faulkner

THE value of hopes and dreams can go down as well as up and you may get back less than you invested. Past performance is no guarantee of future performance.

I learned this in December 2016. My year-overdue sabbatical from ministry was starting. How I needed rest, refreshment, and recharging, after the previous few years. Mum had died in 2014. The following year, we went down from four staff to just me when colleagues unexpectedly left their appointments early. 'Last man standing,' I called myself. Someone had to give hope and be a safe person for shattered church members. 'Just about standing' would have been more accurate. Later that year came a change in responsibilities: I was bereaved of a lovely small church to take on a more challenging one.

The staff losses were why I had to delay the sabbatical. But they—and the other events—were why I desperately needed one.

I was going to catch up on some theology. Reading good theology feeds me. I was going to take some training courses in my hobby of digital photography. Those were the plans.

So much for plans, though. My father's health took a turn for the worse. He was suffering from Alzheimer's disease. As a family, we were going through the first of the two bereavements that condition brings: not the loss of his body in death, but the loss of the personality we loved. Mercifully, he had not become aggressive as some dementia patients do; rather, he had become a naughty teenager again, forever recounting his mischievous antics at grammar school during World War Two.

But Alzheimer's does much more than that. It impaired him from recognising basic bodily signals, from hunger and thirst to balance. The memory loss meant he forgot that he was catheterised. Put these two things together, and he would try to get out of bed to go to the toilet in the night, but would then fall, only to be found by his carer at breakfast time. And that doesn't include the times he decided he wanted to remove the catheter. (I still wince at the thought.)

Thus in the space of one week that December I was called to medical emergencies six times by his carers. I got to know the ambulance crews well. I took to leaving my mobile phone on at night.

My Christmas Day began at 5:25 am. It wasn't the sound of our children waking with excitement, but that of my phone. Dad's voice: 'Dave, I've got a problem.' Another trip to A and E, before being brought back home to his flat. Christmas lunch was Dad and I eating cheese rolls.

In January, he had a serious fall, and the hospital declared it was no longer safe for him to live at home. Three weeks later, he was admitted to a nursing home, where this once shy man started chatting up the pretty young women on the staff, under the influence of his dementia.

My sabbatical never recovered. Most of the photography training didn't happen. I couldn't get my brain to obey orders to study theology. Some niggling chronic health issues worsened, and when I did return to ministry, it was not to the old pattern of morning, noon, and night, six days a week. A nurse told me that could be deadly for me.

On the 1st August 2017, the doorbell rang at 8:50 am, and there stood a police constable. I thought he must have come to ask something of me as a community leader. No. He had called to tell me that Dad had unexpectedly passed away earlier that morning. The man who had given me a love for cricket, rugby, photography, and Tottenham Hotspur was gone. The man who had been the greatest influence on my life apart from Christ was now with his Lord.

Dad's death was the deepest darkness in a period of ever-darkening grey. Now the grey shaded into black. Life became a long trudge of limping along, just about getting the essentials done.

On to December 2017. Advent. And at last a spiritual morsel to feed my hunger for meaning. 'Arise, shine, for your light has come, the glory of the Lord has risen upon you.' 'The people who walked in darkness have seen a great light.' The Advent hope is full of light barging in on the darkness. Angels blaze with light over the shepherds' night-time vigil. A mysterious light performs sat-nav duties for the Magi. John in the beginning of his Gospel writes, 'The light shines in the darkness, and the darkness has not overcome it.' That was it. The coming of Christ was just enough light in the darkness.

It's like the ending to Mark's Gospel. Mark, having almost certainly written his Gospel for Christians suffering persecution for their faith in Rome under the Emperor Nero, writes a measly eight verses about the Resurrection. Just enough light for their darkness.

That's the Advent hope for me: just enough light in the darkness. Sometimes that's all people need.

Just enough light in the darkness. Not only is it sometimes all that people need. For some, it can be all they can handle.

But it's enough.

Dave Faulkner is a Methodist minister in Surrey who blogs on ministry matters at confessionsofamisfit.com. Married to Debbie, he shares a love of digital photography with his daughter and a love of Tottenham Hotspur with his son.

Light of the World

Georgina Tennant

CHRISTMAS doesn't always deliver what the big-budget advertisements promise—wholeness, togetherness, peace. Worse, if it delivers trauma, sadness and loss, it can be hard, in the years that follow, to raise any festive cheer at all.

I swell the ranks of the Christmas trauma-sufferers; my baby was born, without life or breath, in the season of sparkly lights and festive joy. Then, and in the years that have followed, it has been hard to rekindle a love for this incongruent season, as I've navigated the wilderness of loss and healing. Sometimes the pressure Christmas brings for joy and perfection swallows me up as I stand, staring back into the darkness I faced that year.

One thing I have learned to cling onto over the years is the Old Testament verse foretelling Jesus' coming: *The people who walked in darkness have seen a great light; those who dwelt in a land of deep darkness, on them has light shone.* (Isaiah 9:2). He is the Light of the World; His light can drive out whatever darkness we find ourselves facing—past, present or future. I pray that He will ignite something this Advent season—a flicker to a flame, a flame to a roaring fire—to help you emerge from any personal 'land of deep darkness' you find yourself navigating.

When all colour has faded to dull monochrome,
Radiate,
Light of the World

When night comes too soon, and I've wandered from home,
Illuminate,
Light of the World

When shadows press in at the edge of my mind,
Dispel them
Light of the World.

When dawn is far off and hope hard to find,
Rise in me,
Light of the World.

When the gloom of the moment has stolen my song,
Permeate,
Light of the World.

When the dark overwhelms, and the night is too long,
Bring sunrise,
Light of the World.

Rekindle, relight, re-ignite to a flame,
Incandescent,
Light of the World.

Blaze in the dark, 'til the world knows your name,
Unquenchable.

❋

Georgina Tennant is a secondary school English teacher in a Norfolk Comprehensive, who is married with two sons, aged 9 and 7. She loves writing and doesn't get to do it nearly as much as she would like to; her articles and thoughts about life can be found on her own blog (www.somepoemsbygeorgie. blogspot.co.uk), the ACW More Than Writers blog and in local newspapers and magazines.

For Unto Us a Child is Born

Jane Clamp

For unto us a child is born!

WHAT joy is expressed in those few words! It reminds me of the days of telegrams when news of massive importance was conveyed in a few, stark words, punctuated by the word STOP. It conveys completion: the event is accomplished. This is no longer the period of waiting, but the moment the unveiling takes place. What we have dreamed of, longed for, worn out our patience over: whatever we've been expecting, is here.

What do you wait for, still? What promise do you cling to in the sleepless hours when the days have left you exhausted and the nights unrefreshed? Is there a whisper of hope still carried in the wind, ruffling your hair for a moment before moving on and leaving you wondering if you imagined it?

In 1989, God gave me a promise. It was Isaiah 54:13 and I wrote the date in the margin of my Bible. It was a decisive point in my life. Aged 24½, I was considering becoming a mother, looking into the future and imagining the two of us becoming three, and maybe four and who knows how many more? As with everything that has ever mattered to me (and in that category I would sometimes have to include 'finding a car-park space' and 'spotting bargains in the supermarket') I asked God what he thought. If we were better off as we were, then I would learn to be content with that; I just needed to know. This verse in Isaiah shone a torch-beam onto the path, confirming that my idea was also his idea: in fact, of course, he'd had it first. I would be a mother and, more than that, a mother of sons. God said so.

The first son arrived in late September 1990. It all seemed simple—the fulfilment of prayer, promise and pregnancy. Family life settled into a sweet pattern and I was indeed content, for a while. But I knew I wasn't done, and hadn't the Isaiah verse spoken in the plural? I set off down the same path but this time it seemed less well-lit. A few steps in and I started to stumble: one miscarriage after another and another and another, until I found myself looking around at a territory I didn't recognise and whose exit I couldn't find. Re-reading the promise brought little consolation. There were times it seemed to taunt rather than comfort. Nature's act of procreation had defeated me, and my world went black.

Isn't that when the light shines brightest, though, in the midst of deep darkness? It doesn't need to be a 150W spotlight or a dazzling fluorescent strip. If I get up in the night and walk through the lounge towards the kitchen, the room is aglow from the flickering green lights of our Wi-Fi router. In the daytime you would barely register they were there. And so it is with the promises of God: they might seem tiny, hidden amongst the ordinary stuff of life but, when your world is in darkness, they pierce the gloom and push back the shadows.

Now, here's the thing: the son Immanuel, foretold in these verses, hadn't at this point arrived. The words of Isaiah's prophecy have been phrased as if it had already happened but, in fact, it would be a very long time before this child was in his mother's arms. So, it wasn't the actual birth of the baby which caused the people in darkness to see a great light, but the promise of it and the hope within that promise.

Hope is so very difficult to cling to in a season of difficulty. In my own experience, I found it was almost certainly the one thing I couldn't do. If I 'got my hopes up' it seemed there was further to fall when miscarriage occurred and the disappointment overwhelmed me again. As a Christian, there were more layers to the anxiety: I *should* be able to trust, to hope, to keep believing. Why, surely I should know that I was a conqueror!

So, over time, my prayer gradually became, 'Give me the courage to dare to hope,' and God was gentle enough to nod, a smile on his face, and accept that this was all I could manage. Into this dank cave I inhabited, a new word came, this time from Romans 4: *In hope he* [Abraham] *believed against hope.* If Abraham, a patriarch of the Jewish faith, could hope when none existed, then maybe I could try, too. The God who said that a tiny mustard-seed-amount of faith could move a mountain, gave me peace to let me know that my tentative steps towards hope would somehow get me there.

God never wants us to stumble around in darkness. Even when we're going through terrible times, seemingly never-ending and more than we can humanly bear, it is the promise that lights the way. Christmas Day 1996 I held my twelve-day old son in church and sang, *For unto us a child is born, unto us a son is given, and the government shall be upon his shoulders.* I sensed all of heaven joining in the chorus, as on a hillside outside Bethlehem centuries before. God's promise, his unchanging word, had been fulfilled—as it always must.

Jane Clamp is creative writer in residence at BBC Radio Norfolk and on the Thought for the Day team at Premier Radio. She also preaches regularly and speaks at day conferences in which she also ministers through her saxophone playing.

Sharing our Hope

Hannah Robinson

CHRISTMAS is broadly recognised as a time of hope. As
the 25th of December arrives, people tend to feel 'hopeful.'
This doesn't necessarily mean they have a faith connection to the
season, but they see it as a positive family time full of warm fuzzy
feelings with the promise of a new year just around the corner.
Maybe the next twelve months will bring that partner they've
been longing for, a better job, some new friends, a fresh start ...
or not. A new year may bring trials of its own and some of those
hopes could well turn out to be misplaced. In what or whom do
we place our hope, and is our hope worth sharing?

For those of us who do attach spiritual significance to the
celebration of Christ's birth, there can be a feeling of being pulled
in several different directions, ever trying to bridge the sacred/
secular divide—yes we do love Santa and Christmas pudding but
we won't forget to bring the kids to the church nativity service
and play those carols nice and loud when our work colleagues
pop round for a mince pie! Pressures mount up brought on by all
the preparations the festive season entails and the desire to share
why this is truly a time of joyful expectation can feel somewhat
squashed (or non-existent!).

'Hopefulness' at Christmas is so often dictated by
circumstances, and it can be difficult to see beyond them. In
order to appreciate the hope we have as believers, we must strive
to see the bigger picture, acknowledging that true hope in a
loving Heavenly Father brings perspective on all we face and a
peace the world cannot comprehend. Hope exists because there
is darkness, a world full of difficulty and pain and sorrow, and
Jesus came to be a light amidst all of that, a beacon to look to
when so much else is unknown. Christmas provides a wonderful

opportunity to rejoice in this reality and impart it to the wider community.

Many people feel sad at Christmastime because they've lost someone special and it can bring back painful memories. As a university student some 25 years ago I vividly remember my mother's last Christmas before terminal cancer cut short her life several weeks later. The family knew she didn't have much time left and sadness tinged our festivities as we created memories to cherish and cling to when she was no longer with us. As she slipped away we had the precious and certain hope of being reunited in heaven one day, but earthly separations are inevitably desperately hard.

Ten years ago, I experienced my first Christmas as a single mother, feeling a bit overwhelmed as two small kids were looking to me to be the strong one, taking them forward into the next chapter of life. It was a difficult and challenging time but God was with us throughout, blessing us with a wonderful community and loving church family, giving us special memories as we reimagined Christmas in our new reality. When I look at my teenagers I marvel at God's goodness, so apparent in their lives despite a journey that has not always been easy.

Having Jesus as our hope at Christmas is truly something to be shared. The celebration of his birth, an arrival which didn't happen in the easiest of circumstances, is a time when we can bring people to the one who understands the complexity of their lives, the one who is the closest of companions. We live in a world caught up in instant gratification but offering limited long-term fulfilment, leaving so many feeling empty and longing for purpose. People yearn for someone to believe in, but don't always know where to look; Christmas is a wonderful time for believers to share their hope and welcome seekers to come alongside and celebrate with them the 'reason for the season.'

True hope doesn't remove pain but lifts our eyes beyond the here and now, helping us to see a broader reality, a rescue plan for the world that started with a baby in a manger. Sometimes it is only when surrounded by the darkness that we appreciate the light, a light that came to earth 2000 years ago and can never be extinguished. Christ came to bring hope that will never fade.

Above my desk I have a tag with the word 'HOPE' on it, something I brought home from a Christmas day service several years ago. Beside it I have the following scripture, a wonderful promise to hold onto both at Christmas and throughout the year—

'The light shines in the darkness, and the darkness has not overcome it.'

John 1:5

Hannah Robinson is a single mum, with two fab kids, who works in Manchester as an ESOL teacher. She loves everything about Christmas and could happily munch on a mince pie at any time of year!

The Christmas Angel

Jane Anstey

HE slipped into the church after dark, when the congregation had gone. He'd been on the road for a week, and there was nowhere else to go. The church walls would keep out the worst of the cold and damp. Inside it was quiet, and he felt safe for the first time for weeks. He laid his tattered sleeping bag on the stone floor and sat on it, gazing at the decorated Christmas tree with its lights and baubles, and the star at the top that twinkled when he pressed the light switch.

After a while he climbed inside the sleeping bag and lay down. Yet he found himself resisting the sleep that threatened to overwhelm him, in case the dreams came again. Dreams of bombs and guns and knives, and the screams of those they destroyed. Instead he lay remembering his mother's face as she pushed him on to the boat, already overloaded with young men, while behind her his little sisters wept. He would rather have stayed to look after them and taken his chance of execution. Now he did not know what had happened to his family, and his own future looked bleak. From a distance, Europe had seemed a haven of peace and prosperity, a promised land. But the reality was different. Refugees were not welcome, and there were too many of them. He had run from border guards, police, and gangs of smugglers, and he was running still.

'Are you awake?' a child's voice asked.

He opened his eyes. A little girl was sitting beside him. She was about seven years old, with blonde curls and blue eyes—very English.

'The tree is so pretty, isn't it?' she said. He saw that she was dressed in pyjamas under her coat. 'Don't tell anyone, will you? I wanted to spend some time looking at the tree when we were here for the Crib service this afternoon, but we had to go to see Grandpa. I'm supposed to be in bed and asleep.'

He nodded cautiously. He understood English, but if he spoke his accent would betray him.

'Why are you here?' she asked, looking him over more carefully. 'You look very tired. I'm sorry I disturbed you.'

He met her eyes gravely. How innocent she was. How unafraid. As his sisters had been, long ago before the fighting began. Apart from the blonde hair, of course. He smiled.

'That's better,' she said. She fished in her coat pocket and brought out half a packet of biscuits. 'I'm afraid I stole these from the kitchen,' she confessed. 'I thought I might be hungry. Are *you* hungry?' She held out the packet to him.

He took one. It crumbled in his mouth deliciously. He tried to remember when he had last eaten.

A whisper of cold air reached him as the church door opened and a tall man entered. He looked across at the two children by the tree.

'I thought this was where you must be, Angie.' He moved towards them, and the boy shrank away into his sleeping bag. But the face that peered down at him was kindly, and the dog collar reassured him. 'You found a friend, I see.'

The man's voice was deep, and the boy could hear him smile. He felt himself relax, and the feeling of safety returned. The girl nodded.

'He didn't tell me his name, but I don't think he should sleep here tonight. It's too cold. There's plenty of room at the vicarage, though, isn't there, Dad?'

'There is indeed.' Angie's father reached out a hand to the boy in invitation. 'Do come,' he urged. 'You'll be so welcome.'

The boy stared at him.

'My wife died a few months ago,' the pastor went on. There was grief in his voice as well as kindness. 'This might have been a very miserable Christmas for Angie and me. But if you're with us, I know it won't be.'

Thomas hesitated for a moment. Then he got to his feet, rolled up his sleeping bag, and went home with them.

Jane Anstey lives in Cornwall and writes mystery and inspirational romances. Her first novel Beauty for Ashes *was shortlisted for the Romantic Novelists' Association Joan Hessayon New Writers Award in 2007.*

Christmas in the Trenches

Martin Horton

MERRY Christmas, Englishmen.' Did I hear that right? Then it comes again from another German soldier and then another, 'Merry Christmas, Englishmen.'

So, I shout back, 'Merry Christmas.'

Though I don't feel it in my heart. How could I? You would just need to look at this place to realise that Christmas couldn't be celebrated here. This is a place of bloodshed and filth and disease and unspeakable horrors. No. This is not a place for celebrating the birth of the Saviour of the world.

Then suddenly I hear singing. Coming from their trenches.

Stille Nacht, heilige Nacht.

They may be singing in German, but I recognise the tune instantly. It's *Silent Night*, a carol that I know so well, but from midnight mass or round the piano with my family at home. I never would have believed that I'd one day hear it on a battlefield.

Then when they've finished and before I can fully grasp what's happened, one of the lads from our platoon starts singing.

O come, all ye faithful, Jjyful and triumphant.
O come ye, o come ye to Bethlehem.

He's from Wales, the land of song. So, he's got this wonderfully deep rich voice.

Then before I realise it, I'm joining in and other members of the squad are too and not just half-heartedly but we are singing with everything we have got, as though we can cleanse our souls of the horrors of war with this glorious sound and these words of truth.

Then the Germans start clapping. Can you believe it? One

minute there they are trying to blow us to smithereens and next they are applauding our singing.

Then we see lights on the Germans' trench. Not the lights of flares or mortars but gentle candlelight. They'd only gone and put up Christmas trees all along their side. This made me think of the ones I used to have at home which my mother and sister used to decorate so beautifully.

At some point I fall asleep, and what first strikes me the next morning when I awake, is the total and utter silence. No gun fire. No screaming shells. No mortars. Just silence.

All is calm, all is bright.

And all *is bright* too. It was a very heavy frost overnight, so it almost looks as if it has snowed and when the sun hits the frost it's as if there are little glimmers of light everywhere. In some small way it looks beautiful.

We take a peek over the top and see, written on a big placard, over the Germans' side of the trench, the words 'Happy Christmas'.

At that moment one of our officers comes and tells us there'll be no shooting today unless the Germans shoot at us. A one-day truce, as it seems the right thing to do on a day when it should be peace and goodwill to all mankind. Then he wishes us Merry Christmas and off he goes. Well of course we are all delighted. We'd give anything to have a day off fighting hammer and tongs. I'm not sure who started it, us or them but before we know it we are walking in no-man's land. Yes, walking. Not crouching or lying flat on the ground for fear of been shot but actually walking fully upright and then shaking hands with men who mere hours earlier had been trying to kill us. Then we start sharing drinks and cigarettes and photos of sweethearts and laughing and sharing jokes.

Yes, there's lots of laughter but there are moments of sadness too. Seeing soldiers on both sides, taking time to reclaim their comrades. The bodies of their friends, their brothers in arms, and giving them the burial they deserve.

There are so many moments when I could pinch myself, thinking is this really happening? Instead of pinching myself, though, I say a prayer of thanks and pray that I can somehow be a bringer of peace and goodwill to all mankind.

Martin Horton lives in Sheffield with his wife Eva and dog Charlie, a miniature schnauzer, and is the editor of the prayer diary for Wycliffe Bible Translators. He's currently reworking his picture book and enjoying growing as a writer in the process. His other passion is baking, especially meringues!

The Christmas List

A Bittersweet Time to Bring Out the Sherry and Candles

SC Skillman

WHO else finds writing Christmas cards a bittersweet task? I put off 'doing' my Christmas list until I'm in the mood—and light a candle and have a glass of sherry or wine to help create that mood. Why? Because this is the time each year when I must engage with the major changes in people's lives—or certainly the lives of those who are not on Facebook. For the gap of a year between communications throws those changes—for good and for bad—into sharp relief.

There are those who must now be addressed *The X Family*, because a new baby has been born. You remember the mother as a tiny blonde cherub herself.

Then there are the divorces, where you refer back to the previous year's Christmas newsletter and gaze at the photo of the mother with her two tall sons, and remember when you rejoiced at her marriage, at the news of the arrival of their first baby ... and now 'he' has disappeared from their lives and is no longer referred to.

Then there's the lady whose previous husband beat her up—a fact she communicated to you in a Christmas newsletter five years ago—and who sent you the news three years ago that she was marrying someone else to whom she only referred by his first name—and hasn't been in touch since. You'd like to try and restore the lines of communication, but you only have the surname of the ex-husband. You presume she's now living with the new man—unless that relationship too has broken up—but you're not quite sure, and you have to address her in such a way that takes account of different possible scenarios.

And there are the couples whose children have now grown

up and left home and started their own families, so you can now revert to sending cards to the couple alone, without their children's names ... and that feels sad too, despite the fact that this has been in many ways a happy change.

Then there are the people who have died, and whose names have to be crossed off your Christmas list and out of your address book—a task that always feels heartless to me, every time I do it. And the people you're going to send a card to who may well have died, but nobody has told you, so you won't know, unless your card is returned to you by some helpful relative in the New Year.

So much change for good or bad. Then it occurs to me that at least my own family unit is 'the same as last year' and perhaps that fact alone is a cause for at least one small flare of gladness and relief in the hearts of those who receive our greetings.

But should it be? For those on our Christmas list often only communicate the stark facts that will affect the way we address our envelopes to them next year. Behind it all lies the complex reality of their lives.

As a novelist I know what is in my characters' hearts; but not in the hearts of everyone on my Christmas list—the new parents, the recently-bereaved, the freshly-betrayed, the lonely, the divorced, even those who superficially appear to have everything in order, and who claim success and triumph all round for every family member ... their lives are far more complex than can ever be conveyed in the artificial confines of the Christmas card or newsletter.

It has sometimes been said of fiction writers that our greatest joy is when we get to 'play God' to our characters. During an interview with Billy Graham, David Frost remarked that since Billy's God was a God of love: 'Won't God have to let everybody into heaven?' to which Billy Graham replied, 'He doesn't *have* to do anything, if he's God.' I love that reply. And yet, surely this is the essence of God's being: He sees into our inmost hearts. In that truth I find the ultimate light shining into the darkness of our lives.

SC Skillman lives in Warwickshire with her husband David and her son Jamie and daughter Abigail. She has written two suspense novels Mystical Circles *and* A Passionate Spirit, *and a writer's guide,* Perilous Path. *Currently she is seeking a publisher for her new Young Adult gothic novel* Director's Cut *and will soon be publishing another non-fiction book,* Spirit of Warwickshire.

Broken

Howard Webber

I crept up to the broken door
Of the broken cattle shed,
And just across the broken floor
Saw ...
His broken manger-bed.

Even the silence was broken
By a baying, neighing sound;
Even the darkness was broken
As the lamplight shone around.

Even some tears had broken
Down his weary father's face;
Even her heart was broken
Giving birth in so foul a place.

Only one thing remained there
Unblemished, unspoilt, undefiled;
Only one thing was unbroken,
That tiny helpless child.

Yet this child would one day be broken,
Nailed to an old broken tree;
And the one with the hammer and nails?
When I look, I am shocked, for it's me!

Howard Webber's thirty years of ministry as a Salvation Army officer included roles as church leader, itinerant evangelist, church planter and writer. His first book, Meeting Jesus, *won Premier Christianity magazine's coveted Book of the Year award, and was recently followed by his second,* No Longer I? *He and his wife, Judy, are retired and living in Bournemouth.*

For God so Loved the World

Christmas in Every Nation

Finding Christmas

Deborah Jenkins

I DON'T want to be here!' Fighting back tears, I swung the car into a space beside our apartment building. 'There's no Christmas here ...'

The narrow Ankara street echoed with the cries of bread sellers, goats and children. Some of them lifted their heads and eyed us with interest. It was cold. As I unloaded the car, a few flakes of snow wandered down and Pollyanna began to cry. I picked her up, gathered shopping, reached for Matthew.

'Why do we have to stay here for Christmas?' He pronounced it *Cwistmas*.

We inched our way along the pavement with our heavy load. Dismissing his six-year-old honesty, I replied with studied enthusiasm.

'It's more fun here! There's snow!'

He grunted and dragged his feet along the pavement.

As we approached our apartment block, I saw them again, the two boys. Thin and poorly dressed, they waited on the edge of the valley, opposite our apartment. I had often noticed them at this time of day as we returned from school, standing, waiting. I could not read the expression on their faces, but their eyes were hostile, and I did not trust them. Their brooding presence unnerved me.

I felt a familiar rush of panic as we slowed to descend the steps to the front door.

When my husband's travel company suggested a spell in Turkey, I was excited. I knew it would be a fascinating and unusual place to live, and now, eight months on, I had every reason to be happy. We liked our spacious apartment, the children had settled at school, we'd made friends. My Turkish neighbours visited me, bringing gifts, but I somehow couldn't bring myself to like or trust them. Their inquisitive eyes scared me. After a while, I stopped answering the door.

Later, as I stooped to turn on the tree lights, I glanced into the street below. The boys were still there, standing on the pavement in the fading light, waiting. What for? I drew the curtains and turned away.

The next day it began to snow. Huge flakes drifted thickly down, blanketing roofs and thickening roads until the valley was wrapped in silk and silence. I eased the car into its usual space and collected our things while the children played in the snow.

As I groped in my purse for bread money, I wondered if those boys would be there again, my eyes searching the road for them. Yes, there they were: right opposite our building, standing on the pavement, watching us. I paid the bread seller and gathered our things.

'Come on!' I said firmly. 'I'll make hot chocolate.'

The children protested.

'Oh, Mum! Please! We want to play!'

'No!' Out of the corner of my eye, I could see one of the boys moving towards us. My voice rose.

'Now! I want you inside now!' I grabbed their arms and began to run, slipping and sliding on the icy ground.

'Hanimefendi! Madam!' They were calling me, following us. My heart was thudding in my chest as I tried to half pull, half drag the children down the steps towards the main door.

'Wait! Madam!'

But I wasn't waiting for anything. I knew now that they wanted to rob me, hurt me. Perhaps they had a chain, a knife, a gun even. We lurched into the main entrance and began to climb the stairs. In my haste, I tripped and pushed Matthew against the wall. He began to sob quietly.

'Stop it! Hurry up!' I hissed. 'They're coming!'

'Who? Who's coming?' The children looked round, fearfully.

The boys were running up the stairs behind us, shouting in

Turkish. I rammed the key in the lock and wrenched it open, pushing the children through.

But the boys had run fast. The tall one pushed his foot inside the door and levered it open. I screamed.

The boys froze. The tall one stepped out again, watching me strangely and before I could slam the door in their faces, he opened his hand. In it was a 10,000,000 Turkish Lira note. I stared at him, confused. But as I watched, his face broke into a smile.

'Hanimefendi ... yours,' he said. 'In street ... you drop it.'

I gasped. They were returning my money. I must have dropped it when I paid the bread man. 10,000,000 Turkish Lira. Enough to feed a family for a week. I was speechless. We all were. We stood, open-mouthed, watching them. They looked different close-up, softer, friendly almost. Suddenly one of them pointed through the door towards the Christmas tree. He smiled. I saw crinkled eyes and missing teeth.

'Tree!' he said. 'We see ... lights?' He asked this slowly, shyly, uncertain of my response.

'Of course!' Relief made me generous and I ushered them into the front room. I put in the plug and switched on the lights.

The boys sighed with pleasure. Hands by their sides, they gazed in wonder. I noticed their thin clothes and inadequate shoes and thought how cold they must be in this icy weather. But it was only when I saw their solemn eyes reflected in the window beyond, that I realised. It was the lights! They had come every day to see the lights. Not to hurt or steal. But to enjoy the simple pleasure of looking.

I thought I could have no sense of Christmas in this country. But here it was in the eyes of two children and in their empty hands, honest enough to return my money. I thought of my suspicions of yesterday and felt ashamed.

'Mutlu Noel ... Happy Christmas.' I was warm as I showed them out. 'Come again ...'

That night we wrapped up presents to music and lamplight. But we left the curtains open.

'This will be the best Christmas ever,' I said, wrapping the envelope with the 10,000,000 Turkish Lira note in.

And, as I put it under the tree, I glanced out into the waiting darkness. And smiled.

Deborah Jenkins is a writer and teacher from Sussex who writes devotional notes, textbooks and educational articles. Her novella, The Evenness of Things, *is advertised on her blog, at stillwonderinghere.wordpress.com where she writes sporadically about life and other adventures.*

Always Christmas

Lara Akhigbemen

And the angel said to them, 'Fear not, for behold, I bring you good news of great joy that will be for all the people. For unto you is born this day in the city of David a Savior, who is Christ the Lord. And this will be a sign for you: you will find a baby wrapped in swaddling cloths and lying in a manger.'

Luke 2:10–12

I SPENT a couple of years working in the Middle East and the first six months was a shock to my system as I thought I had landed on another planet. As a woman, I wasn't allowed to drive and was advised never to go out unaccompanied. Even if I was allowed to drive, I wouldn't pursue it because their driving requires a whole new skill-set altogether. They drive with phenomenal speed and as if their cars have no brakes. They overtake on either side of cars and cross right in front of another with little or no warning. These are just a few issues.

Visiting restaurants was always interesting. My friends and I always ended up going through the wrong door or ending up at the wrong table or section. What? We were told, 'It's the men's section.' Most times we've ventured into restaurants and other places just thinking—'that will be a nice place to relax or eat', forgetting we don't have the same freedom of choice as we did at home.

Another thing that caught me off guard was the prayer times. During the first few months, the call to prayer woke me early. Around four-thirty or five am. Yes, that early. This I regarded as a call for me to talk to my heavenly Father too. However, during the day, the call for prayer meant almost everything had to come to a standstill, especially in shops, no matter how big or small. In most shops, fifteen minutes before the prayer time customers were not allowed in and those inside were advised to head to the checkout to pay, or to leave and return after the prayer. Customers would start dashing around and picking items as if they were on Supermarket Sweep. I was unfortunate to be in a supermarket checkout queue once at the start of prayer. The checkout was closed and I had to stay in the queue for the duration which lasted about twenty minutes. Sometimes it would last even longer. It is beautiful to see people taking time out to pray, and even at work both colleagues and students did it. I thanked, and still thank, God for the privilege of talking to Him at any time and not having to follow a regimental system.

It is also a region where everyone including the children enjoy the night life. This is due to the very high temperature during the day. At nights, the parks and malls come alive with people shopping, or eating in groups with families and friends including kids playing, until the early morning even on a school night.

Above all, the one thing I couldn't believe wasn't celebrated or acknowledged was Christmas.

Christmas has always been the best season of the year for me. I love the festive atmosphere—the presents, the decorations both at home and in the streets, I look forward to seeing what the high street decorations for the year will be like. I cherish the family gatherings and I can't forget the food; I love preparing and eating it. Moreover, the weather in the northern part of the world—cold and snowy—gives the season a special ambience which I adore.

However, the last two Christmases have been spent in a country where Christmas and Christ are not acknowledged. Before then I never perceived that such places and countries existed on earth. Over the years, I've spent Christmas in various countries in Africa, America and Europe, and the season has always been treated the same. With reverence and respect, with joy, laughter and music in the air. So being in a country where these things weren't happening was upsetting, and quite strange.

Above all, I was working as if it was any other day in the year.

Having pondered on this, a truth I knew deep down became real. Christmas isn't about the gifts, the commercialisation, the festive season and all the other things that come with it nowadays. It's about Christ, the beginning of God's redemptive work for mankind because without the birth, the death of Christ on the cross would have never happened. The birth of Christ shouldn't be remembered only at Christmas; it should be remembered daily with gratitude. Gratitude that God sent his only begotten son to be born like humans, to live and experience what we go through and then die like us; but his death is different, it was a cruel one on a cross. The Bible says, 'And the Word became flesh and dwelt among us, and we have seen his glory, glory as of the only Son from the Father, full of grace and truth'—John 1:14. All these were done so that I might be saved from the clutches of the enemy and eternal death.

I've learnt, no matter where I find myself at Christmas, whether it's celebrated or not, I will celebrate it and remain grateful to God for the process He went through to save me. This last Christmas, I got through the season by reading my Bible, playing carols, reflecting on God's gift to mankind and meeting up with friends after work. For me, it's not a physical experience, it's a spiritual one deeply ingrained in my heart. So no matter where I am and what time of the year—It's always Christmas.

Lara Akhigbemen has been a member of the ACW for a few years. She is an experienced FE tutor who has taught both in the UK and abroad. She has completed her first novel—Facing the Truth (yet to be published) and is working on her second. Based in the West Country, she is a wife and mother.

Christmas with Bethlehem

Mary Mills

'WILL you come to us and share Christmas Day?'
Four bright little faces looked up at me pleadingly.
I accepted their invitation and experienced Christmas, Ethiopian style. It is celebrated on January 6th, when the Orthodox Church celebrates Epiphany—the visit of the Kings to Jesus.

Addis Ababa was full of sheep: herded along the city streets, tied on top of taxis and lorries, still alive, they are kept as fresh as possible until their throats are swiftly cut and they end up in the Christmas cooking pots—if you can afford to buy a sheep. For many it's a chicken—and that is a treat in itself.

I caught a local taxi with my three African 'sons', who act as my body-guards and interpreters whenever I visit Addis. Getting off by the dusty roadside at Kality Village (hardly 'Quality Street'!), we made our way over rough paths, past local shanty shops and homes until we reached the compound of my young friends.

They came out joyfully to greet us—Bethlehem (an appropriate Christmas name, and common for girls in Ethiopia), Moses, Zemen and Kebret. I was ushered into their gloomy mud hut and we perched on the edge of the two bunk-beds, which they share. Their faces glowed—they had company for Christmas!

The hut is spartan, to say the least, but they had made an effort to decorate it. Hanging from the one naked light bulb was a strip of paper cut into a criss-cross pattern. A paper chain. Moses reached up and pulled it off: 'It's for you—a Christmas gift!' It was all he had to give me, and he wanted to give, in the true spirit of Christmas. On closer inspection I noticed that it was a page from a school exercise book, covered in Amharic script. They had cut the pattern out with a razor blade. I told him I would put it up in my home next Christmas to remind me of them. He beamed! A sugar-free, perfect smile.

Looking round their one room, my eyes fell on the 'Christmas tree'—a small branch covered again with exercise-book paper chains. Above it, the words 'Happy Xmars' were written on a scrap of paper and fastened to the wall with a pair of compass points. I made a mental note to send them a small artificial Christmas tree for next year.

We sat on the beds—the only place to sit—and chatted and laughed. I had brought a small box of crackers—a new experience for the children—and they were alarmed and then highly amused by the bangs, and then to find gifts, hats and uninterpretable jokes inside—WOW! Their delight was contagious and the 'happy temperature' rose considerably in that cramped, fetid hut.

After a while, lunch appeared, cooked by Bethlehem, who, at 11 years old, is the 'mother' of the household, their real mum having died a few years ago. The meal was comprised of injera—a flat, spongy, brown pancake-type bread, the staple diet of the country, made from teff wheat. As it was Christmas, it was dressed up with mutton—and memories flooded back to me of the fatty, gristly meat I remember being made to eat as a child. There were lumps of it scattered over the injera. We ate from the same dish, with our fingers. I mentally braced myself and swallowed, whilst trying to put on a good show of enjoying the party fare. They obviously were.

Coffee followed—only there wasn't any, as they couldn't afford it. However, the coffee pot and cups were set out—the coffee ceremony is very important in Ethiopian culture. Bethlehem dressed in her best dress, and with her hair specially plaited for Christmas, presided over the coffee set. Every home must have one. She looked beautiful, and very happy as she posed for a photo.

I had accepted another invitation to the home of the widowed mother of two of my 'minders'. I knew Christmas dinner would be similarly experienced there. But what is squalor and gristly meat compared to the welcome received in those homes?

It was proving a very Happy Christmas, with an abundance of love and joy—and one where I was sharply reminded of the poverty of a stable long ago: *in* Bethlehem …

Mary Mills has been a member of ACW for more than 20 years and has mainly written articles which she hopes will raise awareness—and funds!— for the many in Ethiopia and Uganda with whom she is involved. She is a retired teacher and lives in Barrow-on-Trent with the dog and cat she brought back from Uganda. Her Ethiopian 'son', Moses, (above) now heads up the work they do in Uganda, mainly with disabled and disadvantaged children.

Humbug in Bethlehem

Sean Fountain

I HAVE always had a difficult relationship with Christmas; I find it a difficult time of year. For me, the first strains of Noddy Holder singing 'Merry Xmas Everybody' bring an overwhelming sense of dread. My family treat my dislike with the standing jokes of the 'bah humbug' variety. If I am honest, I do sometimes live up to the joke!

My conceptions of Christmas were, however, challenged very dramatically one year in an experience I will never forget.

I had joined a trip of about forty clergy from different denominations from all over the United Kingdom on a pilgrimage to Israel. It was fairly early January. My friends at home were facing snow and freezing temperatures, we were basking in the warm sun and enjoying good company, great food and some incredible experiences.

There was one day I was wrestling with. Bethlehem. I had such mixed feelings about visiting the place of Jesus' birth. I was expecting something incredibly commercialised, tacky, cheap and nasty. Something that would almost devalue the power and mystery of the incarnation. Coupled with that, we would have to go through 'the wall' something that carves a scar across the face of a beautiful country and divides people. Surely, I thought, this goes against everything that Jesus came for? He was and is the barrier breaker and yet, the place of His birth is a place of nasty division.

My first glimpses of Bethlehem did nothing more than confirm my worst fears. We saw armed guards at the barriers who wished us 'shalom' as they toted their AK-47s. We arrived in Manger Square as Roy Wood and Wizzard belted out 'I wish it could be Christmas every day' from numerous loud speaker systems.

Just as I was about to give up all hope, I approached the Church of the Nativity. The ancient doorway to enter the building is small, about 4ft. It is known as the door of humility, I had to bow to enter. This simple action had a profound effect upon me. I found myself becoming slightly emotional. I began to feel as if God was trying to say something to me through this experience.

Once inside, I got swept along with all of the usual activity that tourists do in the Church. I examined the graffiti made by the Crusader soldiers all those centuries ago. (Whoever thought vandalism was a new concept?) I had Holy Water shaken at me by an Orthodox Priest who then proceeded to wave incense at me—not quite sure what the point of that was, but the faithful seemed to quite like it. I then joined the queue to go and see where, according to tradition, Jesus was born.

It took a little while for my eyes to adjust to the half-light of that underground passage. The press of people, the smell of incense, made quite a heady mixture as I moved with the swell of the crowd. We were swept along toward the star-shaped marker which, some believe, marks the place where Jesus was born. I knelt and, like the others, kissed the spot.

I cannot explain but, even as I write these words, I feel this emotion sweeping over me. I did not want to move from that spot, and had it not been for the crowds pushing and pushing, I might still be there. Was this really the spot where heaven touched earth, where God became man, where the word made flesh was known among us?

As I was moved away I found myself just stopping, turning and looking. Our guide had given us a meeting place and time. As I returned to join my fellow travellers, I felt that somehow things had changed for me. Some of my preconceptions, prejudices and attitudes had been challenged, and deep inside I had been touched by something.

It seemed right that, as a group of pilgrims, we took an opportunity to worship together in the courtyard. We sang 'Away in a manger', we read the story of the shepherds and angels from Luke's Gospel, and then somebody read the prologue from John's Gospel. All of it beautiful. Just as we were preparing to leave, someone suggested that they would like to read 'Christmas' a poem by John Betjeman:

The bells of waiting Advent ring

As I listened to those familiar words, my senses seemed to come to life and I could smell the pine of the Christmas trees of my childhood and could almost taste my mother's homemade mince pies.

My cheeks were wet with tears. I felt an overwhelming sense of nostalgia of missing people who were close to me, of loneliness and hope all mixed into one and the realisation that it was for the mixed up, messed up divided world that God touched this earth in the form of a tiny baby.

Let me move the story on. These events took place in the January, and by the following December, I was preparing for our Christmas festivities in Church and I was having one of my 'bah humbug' moments. As I was putting the finishing touches to yet another carol service, I really felt that I wanted to read the same poem I heard in Bethlehem all those months before.

The following Sunday, as I stood in front of the congregation, I told them the story of what had happened to me in Bethlehem. With only the poem left to read, I found I could only manage the first few words. I stopped. I couldn't read on. The tears were stinging my eyes. As I cleared my eyes and throat, I noticed my tears were not the only ones.

Sean Fountain lives on the Essex Coast and is a minister in a Baptist church. He is fairly new to writing having begun to publish his blog www. fountainsthoughts.co.uk only two years ago. He is married with two adult children and has a grandchild.

Oh, Holy Night

Veronica Zundel

IT was the way my Austrian father did Christmas that gave
me my first taste of the holy—what theologians might call
the numinous. That, and the Anglo-German carol service in the
Chapel of Unity, at Coventry Cathedral, where I first read out
the beautiful Christmas stories, in German, to the congregation.

Don't get me wrong—my Dad wasn't in charge of Christmas
as far as the food went. That was all my Jewish mother, who
took to cooking turkey like a goose to fat, as it were. But because
she hadn't grown up with Christmas, he, raised Catholic with
a Lutheran father, organised all the ritual. And what a ritual it
was. In Austrian tradition, the main celebration was Christmas
Eve, and the tree—a real tree, with real candles in pewter
candleholders clipped on its branches (and we never had a fire)—
wasn't decorated till that morning. Advent, after all, is a period
of fasting and discipline, so you don't celebrate till the end of it.

There'd be a special meal early that evening—I seem to
remember ham (which is neither fasting nor kosher, but we made
our own traditions) and in later years trout sent by air from a rich
Austrian family my parents had befriended, who had a trout farm
as well as gravel pits and a fur trapping company (we never got
sent a fur coat, sadly). Then there'd be a mighty panic and people
rushing all over the house looking for paper, scissors and tape to
do last-minute wrapping, and there was always one present my
mother forgot and had to bring in unwrapped halfway through
(as a refugee family we were short of relatives so had to give each
other lots of presents instead).

And then the silence descended. Once the presents were
all arranged in the lounge in individual piles, we were banned
from the room while Dad lit the candles and played, very softly,

either a record of Austrian carols on his beloved walnut veneer radiogram, or perhaps the same carols on his equally beloved boudoir grand piano. And then he'd ring a bell, and we'd troop into what had magically become a sacred space, where the 'Christkind', the Christ Child (Santa never got a look in) would bring the presents. Once the candles were blown out for safety, we switched off all the lights and waited in the dark for the glow of the four little luminous tree decorations: a lamb, a dove, a cherub and I forget the fourth, though I have them now in my own collection. That moment of ceremony and quiet stayed with me through the years, till I found the real Christ Child for myself and bound myself to him by baptism.

The next day we would have stockings, or rather pillow cases, full of all the presents that had come from outside the family—a welcome, intriguing weight on our feet as we slept. And then Bobby and Hilde, an 'honorary uncle and aunt' with no children of their own (Bobby had been at school in Vienna with my mother) would arrive by train from London—yes, there was public transport on Christmas Day in those days—and we would have our British Christmas dinner. My husband and I still keep this 'double Christmas' with our son, but nothing comes close to the atmosphere my lovely Dad created. And because of him, the Incarnation is still the greatest Christian mystery for me. We would be lost without it.

Incarnation

One might have expected
the earth to shudder and turn blind white;
cities to break down wholesale, their dwellers
scattered into the desert running wide with terror;
one might have expected
sounds mad and damned as mammoths screaming
and hard trumpets blazing limitless judgment;

one might have expected
planets to crumble, worlds burst aflame
stars go off like gunfire, heaven shrink to shreds;
devils to bow homage, angels weep surrender;
one might have expected
anything but this scandalous God entering the world quite
  helpless
simply by being born.

Nativity

Blood on the snow
Mud in the straw
A baby is born
A hundred die
Kings and generals
Speak bullets and bombs
Lines on paper
Move the villages
Towns are christened
Fortunes married
Cities buried
A baby is born
Blood on the snow
Mud in the straw
The poor are still poor
And Caesar still Caesar
World is world
In its common way
And yet in a moment
The world turns over
The womb of a virgin

Is history's span
History itself
Is totally other
Blood on the straw
Mud in the snow
A baby is born.

Veronica Zundel is a professional writer and amateur mother, Mennonite by inclination but without a Mennonite church to go to. She writes regularly for Woman Alive *and for BRF's* New Daylight *Bible notes.*

Miki Investigates Christmas

Nick Watkins

Set in the Philippines, the country with the longest Christmas season in the world.

MACARONI opened his eyes; something was tickling his nose. He flicked it away with his hand.

'Hey bro, why are you slapping my tail?' said Miki, lying next to him.

'Sorry, thought it was a fly.'

He sat up, shading his eyes from the sunlight that was filtering through the branches above.

'Where did you go last night?'

'You'd already fallen asleep when I heard singing coming from the village. I decided not to wake you but to check it out on my own.'

He got up and walked along the branch on all fours, retrieving a small wooden object from a hollow in the trunk.

'What's that in your hand? Did you steal it?' said Macaroni, leaning forward and grasping his hand, 'Let me see.'

'I'll tell you about that later,' said Miki, wrestling his hand loose from his brother's grip. 'Wouldn't you like to know what I found out first?'

Macaroni sat back down again. 'Why were they singing? Tell me everything and don't miss a single thing out.'

'I'm not sure I know what all the fuss was about,' he said, scratching the tuft of reddish-brown fur on his head. 'When I arrived, there was no one left in the houses, they'd all gone to the community hall in the centre of the village. The place was packed and those who didn't get in stood outside, watching through the open sides.'

Macaroni leaned forward, resting his chin in his cupped hands, 'What were they doing in there?'

'That's what I wondered, too. I scampered past the houses towards the hall to take a closer look. Then I saw him: a huge man in red pyjamas and a white beard, staring down at me from a veranda. I was scared stiff I tell you. I froze on the spot.'

Macaroni smiled. 'He must have been hot in that outfit. Did he say anything?'

'Well, that was the strange thing; he didn't say a word or move a muscle. Then it came to me, he wasn't real—he was made of cardboard. Maybe, I thought, this was the person they were singing about.'

'What happened next?'

'Once I'd got over the shock of the man in red pyjamas, I continued towards the hall and hid behind a house post to watch. A man in a robe at the front of the hall lifted a big silver cup high above his head; he was chanting something. Behind him was this giant cross-shaped piece of wood.'

'That doesn't really help us understand what was going on,' said Macaroni wriggling his bottom. 'Were they singing to the silver cup? Where does the cross fit in? I wish we understood the sounds they make, it would make living next to them so much easier.'

Miki was enjoying telling the story; for once, he was the one talking and his brother the one listening. 'I found out more when I headed back home through the village. Hanging from the roofs of many homes were these star-shaped decorations. The frames were made of bamboo sticks covered with coloured tissue paper with a light in the centre. I've never seen the village look so colourful before.'

'This doesn't make any sense at all,' said Macaroni blowing air out through his lips. 'What do those stars have to do with the cross or the man in red pyjamas?'

Miki held up one hand in mock imitation of the village teacher he had seen the day before. 'But it gets even more complicated.

On one veranda I saw a miniature house with a thatched roof but no walls. Inside it the owner had placed carved figures standing around a cot with a tiny wooden baby in it.'

Macaroni frowned and stood up, his long tail moving restlessly behind him. 'So it could be about that human baby. But why would anyone—human or monkey—do that? Our baby brother is cute, and annoying, but we don't sing about him.'

'Anyway, that brings me back to this,' said Miki opening his fingers to reveal the small wooden figure in his palm. 'This is the wooden baby I told you about. Take a look.'

He handed the figure to his older brother, who held it close to his eyes. 'Doesn't look much to me. Baby monkeys are far cuter.'

Miki shook his head. 'These humans are fascinating creatures but I don't think we'll ever understand them.'

'No, we won't, but that doesn't allow us to steal from them, does it? You'll have to return this later when it gets dark.' He reached for his brother's hand, gently opened his fingers and placed the wooden baby into his palm.

Nick Watkins was born in Bristol, is married to a Finn, worked for fourteen years as a church planter in the Philippines and served as a pastor in the UK until his retirement in 2015. He now volunteers and writes.

And Finally

Why?

Shelley Spiers

Why did a manger hold Heaven's King?
Why did shepherds bow and angels sing,
As a baby lay in a cattle shed?
For God so loved the world.

Why did a cross hold the sinless one?
Why did nails pierce the hands of God's own Son,
As a crown of thorns adorned his brow?
For God so loved the world.

Why was he placed in a borrowed grave?
Was this not the one who had come to save?
A promised Messiah and Conquering King?
For God so loved the world.

Why were grave clothes folded where once he lay?
Why was the stone rolled away?
So that we can see that he is risen!
For God so loved the world.

Why will heaven one day be my home?
Because my Saviour is on the throne.
My sin debt is paid by the one without sin.
Clothed in his righteousness, I stand forgiven,
For God so loved the world.

For God so loved the world, that he gave his only Son, that whoever believes in him should not perish but have eternal life.

John 3:16

Shelley Spiers is a primary school teacher from County Armagh, Northern Ireland. In her spare time she enjoys reading, playing the piano, writing songs and telling children about Jesus.

Good News

Christina Clark

And so, the Lord, Creator, King of Kings
Gave up His Right to sit upon High Throne;
Relinquished rule of man, and Time, and things
To put on flesh—
        Call His Creation 'Home'!

So, bound by rules that He Himself had made
Became a babe, and on mere flesh relied—
Grew up, a humble man, and learned a trade;
He studied; lived and loved; He laughed and cried.

This God-Man, Jesus, man and God combined
So truly regal, yet so humbly man –
He walked this earth, to His own death resigned
To bring about The Great and Glorious Plan;

The Great Good News, by Prophets long foretold;
Redemption for the sinners, saved by grace –
Revealed by Angels, and to Shepherds told,
And marked by stars revolving high in space.

To Kings and Shepherds, status high and low
By different ways this News was shed abroad –
And still we're urged by Heaven—up and go
To spread the News that Jesus Christ is Lord.

Christina Clark is a committed Christian, wife and mum. She has written poetry since she was at primary school but this is her first published work.

A Christmas Prayer

Dawn Wedajo

FATHER God, we thank You for the miracle of Christmas and for giving us the precious gift of Your only son Jesus, born of a virgin so long ago. Truly there was a place in time when love came down wrapped up in a baby, a holy child of great majesty, heaven's finest, yet born without worldly honour or splendour in a lowly stable. We thank You, Lord, for selfless agape love and gracious humility.

We thank You for Mary and Joseph, His courageous earthly parents, who journeyed to Bethlehem: no doubt weary and tired without the trappings of home, seeking refuge, looking for somewhere to stay, but having enough faith to trust and totally depend on You, knowing that somehow Your purpose would be accomplished far beyond their view or understanding.

We thank You for wise men from the East and faithful shepherds guarding their charges who were willing to step out of their daily routine to follow Godly instruction and pursue the promised Messiah.

We thank You, Lord, that because You gave us Jesus, the world would be changed for ever. We rejoice in the knowledge that we have a Saviour: may our hearts be stirred as never before as we lift up Your name. We know that the path at times can be difficult, hard to bear or comprehend but, like those who have gone before, may we hold on to Your word and put our trust in You, with the blessed assurance of victory in Christ Jesus.

We pray that as we come together with our families and friends and celebrate this Christmas season, we will never forget Your sacrificial gift and that we will share with others the greatest story the world has ever known.

Amen.

ʌn is a busy mother of two and a freelance writer, her work has appeared n a variety of magazines. She is currently in the process of completing a children's book.

Editors

WENDY H JONES

Wendy H Jones is President of the Scottish Association of Writers and the author of the highly successful, award winning, crime series *The DI Shona McKenzie Mysteries*. She also writes *The Fergus and Flora Mysteries* and *Cass Claymore Investigates*. Her recent foray into children's picture book writing led to *Bertie's Great Escape*, published in October 2018. After having a career in the Military, she moved into Academia, where she wrote for academic publications and textbooks. She has had extensive marketing training throughout her career. After a period of illness she moved back to her native Scotland where she settled in Dundee. This led to her career as an author. She is the founder of 'Crime at the Castle', Scotland's newest crime festival, presents *Wendy's Book Buzz Radio Show*, on Mearns FM and is a partner in 'Equipped to Write', a training and coaching company. A popular public speaker, she has spoken at many conferences and events, both in the UK and internationally.

AMY ROBINSON

Amy Robinson is a writer, performance storyteller and ventriloquist, and the children's worker in her benefice. She has written three books about puppetry and storytelling, published by Kevin Mayhew, and provides scripts and materials for GenR8, a Cambridgeshire charity running Christian assemblies and events in schools. She co-founded the storytelling company Snail Tales, with which she still writes and performs. In her spare time, she writes poetry and makes attempts at novels. She lives in a rectory in Suffolk with the rector, two children, two guinea pigs and too many puppets to count.

…MP

…lamp is the author of *Too Soon*, a mother's journey through …iscarriage (SPCK). As an interior designer, she has a heart for restoration of both buildings and people which she reflects in her writing. She writes and broadcasts for local radio and is on the *Thought of the Day* team at Premier Christian Radio. She contributes regularly to an online Bible commentary and blogs for the ACW. Jane is Groups' Coordinator for the ACW and leads the Brecks, Fens and Pens ACW group in West Norfolk.

Find Out More

Website:
http://www.christianwriters.org.uk

Twitter:
https://twitter.com/ACW1971

More Books
New Life: Reflections for Lent was released in March 2018

Lightning Source UK Ltd.
Milton Keynes UK
UKHW04f1215181018
330767UK00001B/3/P